Simply
PCs

Bob Albrecht

Osborne **McGraw-Hill**
2600 Tenth Street
Berkeley, California 94710
U.S.A.

Osborne **McGraw-Hill** offers software for sale. For information on software, translations, or book distributors outside of the U.S.A., please write to Osborne **McGraw-Hill** at the above address.

Simply PCs

1234567890 DOC 998765432

ISBN 0-07-881741-2

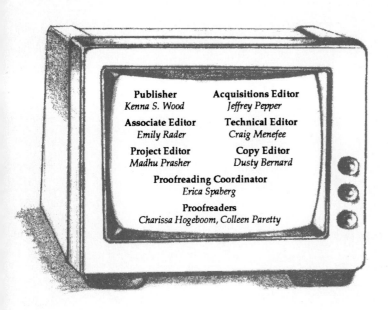

Publisher
Kenna S. Wood

Acquisitions Editor
Jeffrey Pepper

Associate Editor
Emily Rader

Technical Editor
Craig Menefee

Project Editor
Madhu Prasher

Copy Editor
Dusty Bernard

Proofreading Coordinator
Erica Spaberg

Proofreaders
Charissa Hogeboom, Colleen Paretty

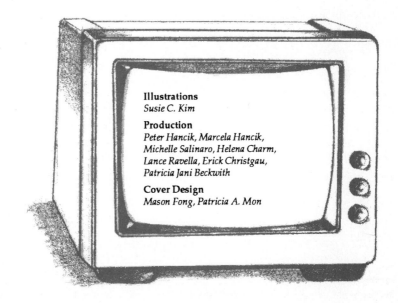

Illustrations
Susie C. Kim

Production
*Peter Hancik, Marcela Hancik,
Michelle Salinaro, Helena Charm,
Lance Ravella, Erick Christgau,
Patricia Jani Beckwith*

Cover Design
Mason Fong, Patricia A. Mon

Contents

The author invites you to try the *Tightwad Computer Gazette*, a newsletter about getting the most computer for the least money. In the gazette, your guides will be Tightwad Thomas, Cathy Collegian, Sandra Salesperson, Andy Arcade, and others.

In the spirit of frugality, the first issue is free. To get your copy of the gazette, send a SELF-ADDRESSED, STAMPED (29-cent) ENVELOPE to:

Tightwad Computer Gazette
P.O. Box 62
Graton, CA 95444

It's Simple to Use This Lay-Flat Binding . . .

Open this book to any page you choose and crease back the left-hand page by pressing along the length of the spine with your fingers. Now, the book will stay open until you're ready to go on to another page.

Unlike regular book bindings, this special binding won't weaken or crack when you crease back the pages. It's tough, durable, and resilient—designed to withstand years of daily use. So go ahead, put this book to the test and use it as often as you like.

What Is a Personal Computer?

A *personal computer*, or *PC* for short, is an electronic appliance that processes information. You probably have other electronic appliances in your home, like a microwave, a telephone answering device, or even electronic home office equipment such as a facsimile (fax) machine. Most homes also have several electronic entertainment appliances: audio cassette recorders, compact disc (CD) players, video cassette recorders (VCRs), and televisions and radios. Collectively, these devices can be called *hardware*.

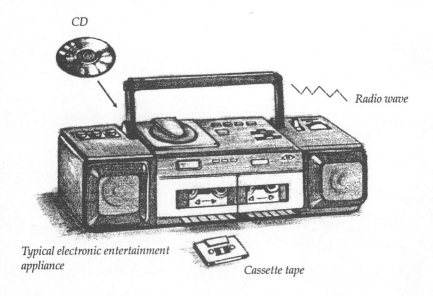

CD

Radio wave

Typical electronic entertainment appliance

Cassette tape

Entertainment hardware devices play, and sometimes record, information found on a particular type of *medium*. The content of what is found on audio/visual and computer media is referred to as *software*. For example, an audio cassette recorder plays from, and records onto, a cassette tape (the medium). The content of an audio tape cassette (the software) might be music, speech, or other sounds.

A CD player plays a compact disc (the medium) whose content (the software) might be music, speech, other sounds, or images. A VCR plays and records video images and sounds (the software) by using a video tape (the medium). Televisions and radios tune into broadcasted signals (the medium) and turn those signals into images and sounds (the software).

A personal computer (PC) is a "smart" electronic hardware device that is adaptable to a wide range of information-processing tasks.

A PC can be used to manipulate many forms of information (text, numbers, graphics, music, sounds, moving images). You direct a PC to perform particular tasks by running *programs* (software) that tell the PC what to do. For PCs, programs are usually stored on a form of computer medium called a *disk*. The following table lists several appliances and the medium and software associated with each hardware unit.

Hardware	Medium	Software
Audio cassette player	Cassette tape	Music, speech, sounds
Compact disc (CD) player	Compact disc	Music, speech, sounds, images
Video cassette recorder (VCR)	Video tape	Images and sound
Television	Airways	Images and sound
Radio	Airways	Music, speech, sounds
Personal computer (PC)	Disk	Programs

Hardware Components of Typical PCs

PCs come in many shapes and sizes. However, when you look at different PCs, you often find that they have similar hardware components. For example, a typical PC has a keyboard, a monitor, a chassis or box-like unit that contains the computer circuitry, one or more disk drives, a collection of cables and power cords, and usually a pointing device and an attached printer.

The PC *keyboard* looks similar to the keyboard on a typewriter, with a few additional keys. The PC *monitor* looks like a television

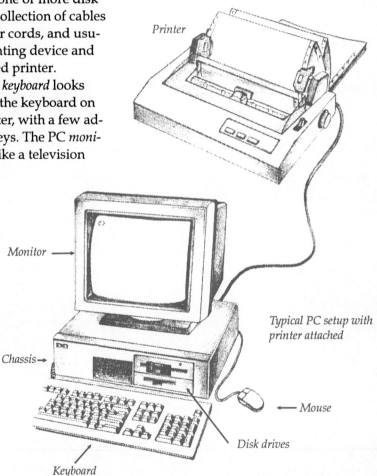

Printer

Monitor ⟶

Typical PC setup with printer attached

Chassis ➡

⟵ *Mouse*

Disk drives

Keyboard

screen. The *chassis* on a PC is generally box-shaped and flat on top, providing you with a convenient place to set the monitor. The front or side of the chassis may have one or more slotted openings that let you know the locations of the computer's *disk drives*. *Pointing devices* attach to the chassis. They let you direct actions on the PC's monitor without touching the keyboard. The most common PC pointing device is called a *mouse*. For a typical PC setup, the printer sits near the PC and is connected to the PC chassis by a cable.

Laptop and Notebook PCs

Two trends continue to hold true as new personal computers are being made: PCs are getting smaller and more compact, and PCs are becoming more powerful. Innovations in the design and manufacturing of hardware components have created several new categories of PCs based on their size and portability.

First came *laptop PCs*. Laptops reduced the size and weight of PCs by integrating the keyboard and the monitor into the chassis unit. The large, external PC monitor became a flat screen inside the top of the lap-sized PCs. Laptops weighed in at between 10 and 20 pounds.

Recently, a proliferation of smaller, lighter weight (4- to 7-pound) PCs called *notebook computers* arrived. Notebook computers combine the advantages of small size, light weight,

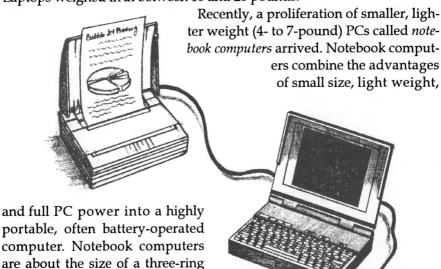

and full PC power into a highly portable, often battery-operated computer. Notebook computers are about the size of a three-ring binder.

The size and portability of peripheral hardware components, such as printers, have also been affected. For example, you can now buy a high-quality, lightweight (4-pound), battery-operated printer to use with your PC. These printers are roughly the size and weight of a notebook PC.

How PC Hardware Units Work Together

The PC keyboard is your control center. By pressing keys on the keyboard, you enter information into the computer and tell the PC what to do. The typical PC keyboard looks like a typewriter keyboard with three sets of additional, special-purpose keys called function, control, and numeric keypad keys.

The keyboard has ten or more *function keys* labeled F1, F2, and so on. Function keys are also referred to as *soft keys, programmable keys,* or *F-keys*. These keys

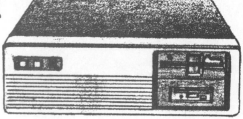

perform different operations depending upon the software you are using.

Control keys are used to control various computer actions. Examples of control keys found on most PC keyboards are INSERT, DELETE, BACKSPACE, and a few other keys whose names are on the keys. The names of control keys are often abbreviated on the keyboard. For example, Insert might be INS, Delete might be DEL, and Backspace might be either BKSP or a left-pointing arrow.

The *numeric keypad keys* are arranged like the keys on an adding machine. You may use the numeric keypad to enter groups of numbers.

Each time you press a key on the keyboard, a signal is sent to the computer circuitry housed in the PC chassis. The computer's *central processing unit* (or *CPU*) decodes the incoming signal and, based on the program being used, decides what to do. The CPU is also called the PC's *microprocessor* or *microprocessing unit.*

If you press a function key, the CPU looks up the action assigned to the pressed key and takes that action. If you press a control key, the CPU initiates the indicated control task. If you press a key on the regular keyboard, the CPU displays a number, letter, or punctuation symbol on the PC's monitor. The CPU may also store what you typed into the PC's *memory* or onto a disk in one of the computer's disk drives. PCs have two main types of memory circuits: *RAM* (random-access memory) and *ROM* (read-only memory).

To use a PC productively, you do not need to know how the CPU, RAM, and ROM interact with the monitor, disk drives, and programs. In fact, you may never need to open the PC's chassis and look at its circuitry. You only need to know that when you press a key, you tell the program and CPU to take an action. Eventually, you learn to press sequences of keys to accomplish the tasks you want done.

When the CPU displays information, what you see is determined by the type of PC monitor you are using. Monitors come in a variety of sizes and support a variety of features.

Monitors vary in size from 9 to over 25 inches. Larger monitors display larger but not always sharper images. The sharpness of an image is determined by the *resolution* of the monitor. High-resolution monitors create sharp images but tend to cost more than low-resolution monitors.

Monitors also come in monochrome or color. *Mono- chrome monitors* display infor- mation in a single color against a contrasting colored

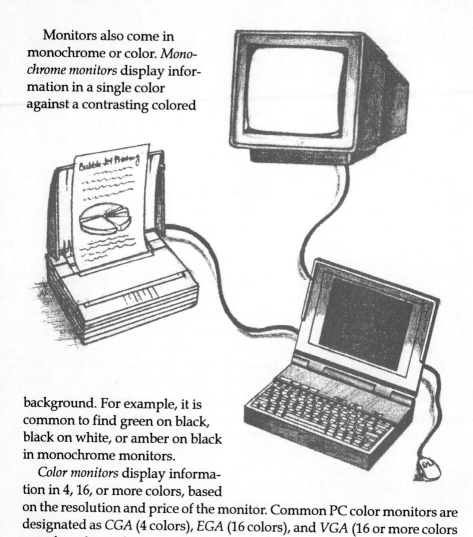

background. For example, it is common to find green on black, black on white, or amber on black in monochrome monitors.

Color monitors display informa- tion in 4, 16, or more colors, based on the resolution and price of the monitor. Common PC color monitors are designated as *CGA* (4 colors), *EGA* (16 colors), and *VGA* (16 or more colors out of a palette of many colors).

Monitors can be used to display *graphics* (images) as well as text and numbers. To display graphics, your PC must be able to generate the graphics images and you must have a monitor that matches the type of images that the PC generates. Most PCs rely on a *graphics board,* a separate circuit board that is installed in the PC's chassis, to display images.

Communications among a PC's hardware units is done by means of cables.

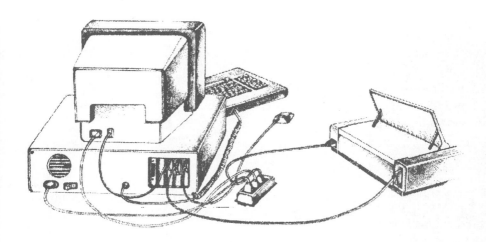

If you look carefully at the PC chassis, the monitor, and the printer, you will find on each an on/off switch. You will also find a power cable receptacle and one or more plug locations, called *ports*. The unit with the most ports is the chassis. The keyboard, the monitor, printers, and pointing devices all connect to specific ports on the chassis.

Laptop and notebook computers also have ports for external monitors, printers, pointing devices, and other hardware.

Printers

The printer you connect to your PC lets you print on paper the images and information you see on your monitor. The three most common types of printers are dot-matrix, ink-jet, and laser printers.

Dot-matrix printers provide a low-cost way to produce documents with letter-quality (LQ) or near-letter-quality (NLQ) characteristics. These printers print each character by selecting a set of dots within a rectangular array, or *matrix*. The total number of dots used in the matrix determines the quality of the printed image.

Ink-jet printers use electrically charged streams of ink particles to create dot-matrix printed images. Ink-jet printers tend to be quieter than

Commonly used dot-matrix printer

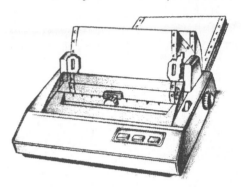

Example of portable ink-jet printer

conventional dot-matrix devices since the ink-jet does not use a printhead that strikes the paper.

Laser printers produce high-quality documents. Laser printers support the "what you see is what you get," or *WYSIWYG* (pronounced "wizzy-wig"), phenomenon associated with desktop publishing (DTP).

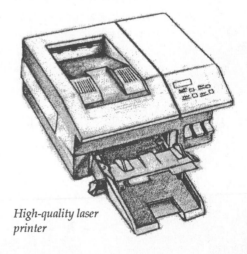

Laser printers rely on the same technology used in copy machines. With a high-resolution monitor and a laser printer, you can turn your PC into a local publishing operation. What you see on your

High-quality laser printer

monitor can be printed on paper and used by a regular print shop as camera-ready material. Laser printers have radically changed design, typography, and print production businesses.

Of the three types of printers, laser units are the most expensive and produce the highest quality documents. Because they print an entire page at once, laser printers are faster than ink-jet or dot-matrix devices.

Pointing Devices

A pointing device lets you direct a computer's actions by "pointing" to a specific area on the monitor. Pointing devices extend the actions that you can perform with the keyboard alone. For example, with effort, you may be able to draw an image on the monitor by using just the keyboard keys. But with a pointing device, that task becomes easier. You are freed to focus on the aesthetics of what you are creating.

Today's common PC pointing devices include the mouse, the trackball, and the pen and tablet unit.

A *mouse* is a palm-sized device with a ball on the bottom that you roll around on a flat surface.

A mouse

As you move the mouse, an indicator on the monitor also moves, corresponding to where you move the mouse. A mouse may have from one to three *buttons* on its top surface. You use the buttons to let the computer know when you wish to take specific actions.

A *trackball* is like an upside-down mouse.

A trackball has a ball on top of the unit, along with one or more buttons. Instead of moving the unit around, you use your fingertips to move the ball. When you move the ball, an indicator on the monitor

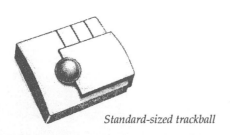

Standard-sized trackball

moves as well. Trackballs are
handy in confined work spaces
where a mouse cannot be easily
used. Specially designed, smaller
trackball devices are available for
use with portable PCs.

*Trackball for a notebook
computer*

Pen and tablet systems use a pen
or stylus as the primary pointing
instrument. *Light pen systems* let
you place the end of the pen directly on the monitor. The computer detects the location of the
light pen and directs the actions of the program. Other pen systems rely
on a sensitized *tablet* or *pad* that sits on the table next to the PC.

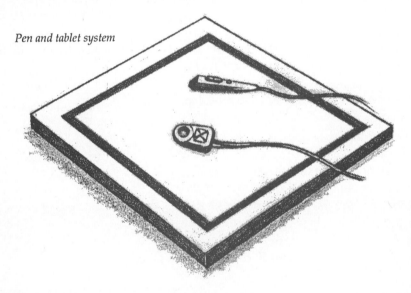

Pen and tablet system

With these systems, you place the end of the pen or stylus on or above
the pad. The computer detects the location of the pointing device and
follows your actions. If you move the pen, the computer moves an indicator
on the screen. If you draw a line on the tablet, a line appears on the monitor.
If you use the pen to point to an action to be taken, the PC performs the
task.

What Can You Do with a PC?

PCs are hardware devices that run programs (software) and process information. Programs are prepackaged sets of instructions that tell a PC how to perform a task. Programs are stored on computer media called *disks*. Programs use and create collections of data, called *files*, that are also stored on disks.

PC Disks and Disk Drives

Before you explore what a PC does when it runs programs, it is helpful to know about disks and PC disk drives.

Floppy Disks and Drives

The front or side of a PC has one or more slots where its floppy disk drives are located. The slot at the opening to the drive lets you insert and remove disks when you are using the PC. For this reason, floppy disks are referred to as removable media. Floppy disk drives, and the disks that you put into those drives, come in two sizes: 3 1/2-inch and 5 1/4-inch. The 3 1/2-inch floppy disks are enclosed in a rigid plastic case. The 5 1/4-inch disks are covered with a soft, flexible, protective cover. Inside each case is a shiny, disk-shaped piece of thin plastic. Information is magnetically stored onto and retrieved from this thin plastic disk.

3 1/2-inch disk

5 1/4-inch disk

Floppy disks are like tiny filing cabinets that hold lots of information. You can easily carry several disks around in one hand.

Hard Disks and Drives

PCs may also have a type of disk drive called a *hard disk drive.* If your PC has a hard disk drive, you may see nothing on the chassis to indicate the location of the drive except a small, red "ready" light. The light turns on when the hard disk is being used.

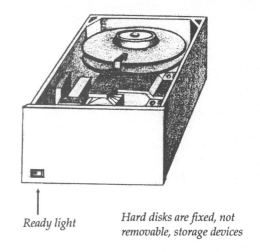

For a hard disk, you will see no slot on the chassis where disks are inserted and removed. Unlike floppy disks, which are removable media, a hard disk is normally a *fixed* media device; the disk remains inside the PC or the hard disk drive case. If the hard disk is inside the PC chassis, it is called an *internal disk drive.* If the hard disk is in a box connected to the chassis, it is referred to as an *external disk drive.*

Ready light

Hard disks are fixed, not removable, storage devices

Hard disks have two major advantages over floppy disks: they are faster and they store a lot more information. The smallest capacity hard disk drives store as much data as found on 20 to 50 floppy disks. Larger hard disks may store as much data as found on hundreds of floppy disks.

How fast is a hard disk drive when compared to a floppy disk drive? About 100 times as fast when storing and retrieving information! Using a hard disk can significantly enhance your productivity when you use a PC.

How Much Data Fits on a Disk?

Information being stored or used on a PC is often measured in terms of a number of characters. This concept is easily understood if you consider that a full single-spaced typed page contains about 3000 characters. This count includes the spaces between words, punctuation marks, and any special symbols.

Based on the PC being used, a typical 5 1/4-inch PC disk stores either 368,640 or 1,213,952 characters. This means that with some PCs, you can store up to 400 full pages of text on this size disk. A typical 3 1/2-inch disk stores either 737,280 or 1,457,664 characters. This means a single 3 1/2-inch disk may store up to 480 text pages. This entire book could be stored easily on a single floppy disk with room left over.

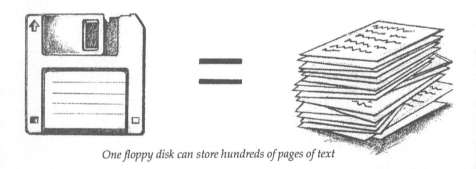

One floppy disk can store hundreds of pages of text

The smallest hard disk stores about 20 million characters, or around 14 to 16 times as much as a high-capacity floppy disk. This size hard disk could then store nearly 7000 pages of text.

PC users refer to the size of a disk in terms of an approximate number of characters that is slightly less than the actual number. The symbol K or M is placed after each number, where K stands for "thousands" and is pronounced "kilo," and M stands for "millions" and is pronounced "mega." Often the computer term "byte" replaces the word "character" and the letter B is placed after the K or M. Consequently, you will hear PC users talk about *kilobytes* (KB) of storage or *megabytes* (MB) of memory.

Disk Type	Disk Size	Capacity in Bytes	Pages of Text
Floppy	5 1/4-inch	360KB or 1.2MB	120 or 400
Floppy	3 1/2-inch	720KB or 1.44MB	240 or 480
Hard	Varies	20MB and up	7000 and up

Software

You can use a PC to help with a variety of information processing tasks. You can use it to create and print documents. You can use it to organize lists of information such as address books and inventories. With a PC, you can perform financial calculations and organize your tax data. You can use a PC to help draw and refine graphics images. PCs can be used for education, recreation, and communications. Just about anything you now do with paper and pencil can also be done using a PC.

To direct a PC in performing a specific task, you use one or more software programs or applications. Programs are prepackaged sets of instructions, stored on disks, that tell the PC how to perform a task.

PC software programs can be grouped into the following nine application categories: writing and editing programs, financial packages, database management systems, graphics programs, desktop publishing packages, education programs, entertainment packages, communications programs, and utility programs. Almost everything you will ever want to do with a PC can be done by using one or more programs that fall into these categories.

Writing and Editing Programs

Perhaps the most frequently used application on a PC is *word processing*—the creation, preparation, editing, and printing of documents. Word processing programs, or *word processors*, as they are called, let you type and edit documents ranging from a personal letter to an entire book.

Unlike typewriters, word processors assist with the correction of mistakes, the insertion and deletion of blocks of text, and the movement of text within a document. Some word processors help correct misspellings, give you control of the format and style of documents, and let you choose the appearance of the printed information.

Example word processing screen

When you use a word processor, what you type appears on the monitor, where you can edit and make corrections. Once you finish typing and editing, you can print what you see on the screen to paper. Computer-printed materials are referred to as *hard copy*.

Financial Packages

PC financial packages include special-purpose programs that help balance checkbooks, assist with budgets, and perform specific financial calculations. More complex financial programs assist with financial planning and management tasks, prepare tax returns, make wills, and help run businesses.

The most used of all financial packages have been spreadsheet programs. Electronic spreadsheets, dynamic, screen-based calculation sheets, have virtually replaced the type of ledger sheets commonly used by planners and accountants.

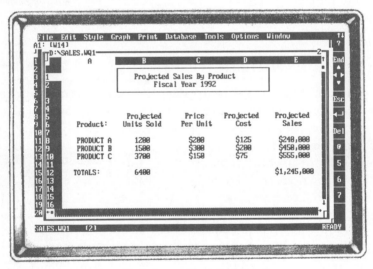

Typical spreadsheet display

PC spreadsheet users have discovered that they can customize electronic spreadsheets to fit personal and business financial needs. By changing numbers in a spreadsheet and making instantaneous recalculations, users can evaluate many alternatives. With the press of a key, spreadsheets provide immediate answers to numerous "What if?" questions.

Database Management Systems

If you have to manage large lists of information, you can probably make good use of a PC database management program. A *database management system (DBMS)* lets you create, edit, sort, retrieve, and print information.

With a database program, you can search through data, extract parts of the database, and often design and print customized reports. Many database programs include print features that let you create mailing labels and help you produce form letters.

Database management systems are used to organize and display information

Most DBMS programs also let you store selected data on a disk in formats that can be used by your word processor or spreadsheet program. In fact, PCs now have several *integrated software packages* that include a word processor, spreadsheet, and database management system in a single program. The main feature of an integrated package is that data created in one part of the package can be easily used in another part. For beginning PC users, integrated packages work well as both learning and productivity tools.

Graphics Programs

One of the most fascinating features of a PC is its ability to display graphics images on the monitor. A host of PC graphics programs now exist to assist with the tasks of designing, drawing, painting, rendering, and animating images.

When you create images by using a graphics program, you generally do so with a pointing device such as a mouse, a trackball, or a pen and tablet system. The art you create in a graphics program can be used within other programs such as word processors and desktop publishing packages.

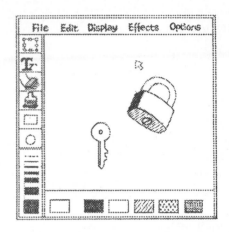

The workscreen for a typical graphics program

With a desktop publishing package, you can create professional-looking documents

Desktop Publishing Packages

Desktop publishing packages help you create professional-looking documents and publications. Desktop publishing programs let you combine text, graphics, and design elements into pages that are ready to be printed by a regular print shop.

If you plan to produce a newsletter, a small paper, brochures and flyers, or greeting cards, you may want to investigate the PC's desktop publishing packages. PCs and desktop publishing have changed forever how print products are being created and published in homes, schools, and businesses.

Education Programs

People use educational software for learning all kinds of things. There are hundreds of PC educational programs that can be used to learn the basic "three R's."

Programs exist that teach language arts, mathematics, science, social studies, and dozens of other topics. Whatever your interest, you can probably find a PC educational program that meets your needs. Many educational programs are fun to use and fit into the software category called "entertainment packages."

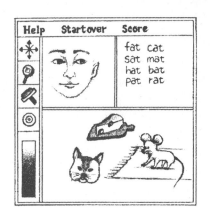

Learning with a PC program can be fun

Entertainment Packages

One of the largest groups of PC software is entertainment programs. You will find that there are hundreds of PC entertainment programs.

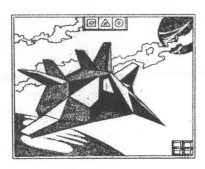

*PC games provide hours of
entertainment and challenge*

Types of entertainment packages range from arcade-style programs, to strategy games designed to test your ingenuity and creative problem-solving skills, to simulations that include both standard and nonstandard card and board games. Increasingly, software that combines good education and entertainment is changing how people learn, in schools and in the home.

Communications Programs

Communications programs (or telecommunications programs) and a hardware device called a *modem* let you send and receive information with your PC. The PC or computer you are sending to or receiving from may be in the next room, down the block, or across the world.

The connection between the computers is made through the modems by using telephone lines between the two locations. In effect, one PC "calls" the other PC, and they "talk" to each other by using the modems to help send and receive the "conversation."

Utility Programs

A host of PC utility programs exist to help make your sessions at a PC more productive. For example, there are PC utility programs that help you manage and catalog your disk files. Other utilities assist with PC house-keeping tasks or speed up specific PC operations, thus freeing your time for more productive activities.

Other utilities let you examine a disk of graphics images and display the images on the PC monitor as if you were looking at a photo album. Some utility programs come with your PC system; others may be purchased separately, based on your particular computing needs.

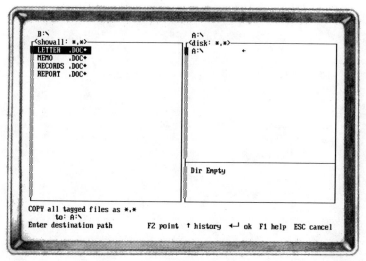

Typical utility program display

Selecting Software for Your PC

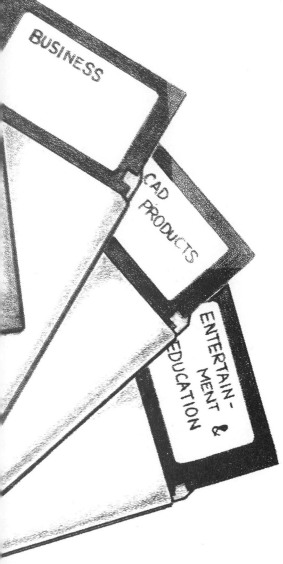

BUSINESS

CAD PRODUCTS

ENTERTAIN-MENT & EDUCATION

Before you run out and purchase a PC, you may want to spend some time doing the following:

1. Create a list of the tasks you expect a PC to do for you, both now and in the future.

   • Will you be writing letters only, or writing everything from letters to books?

   • Will you be drawing images on the PC and putting those images in your documents?

   • Do you need help with financial calculations?

   • Do you plan to use your PC as an entertainment device?

   • Will your PC be used in a home office or home business environment?

   • What about using your PC as a learning tool?

2. Investigate which software programs are available to perform your tasks. Resources you might use to help gather information about software packages are PC magazines, local computer stores, PC user groups, and friends who own PCs. If possible, obtain hands-on experience with programs before you buy anything. Local  schools and colleges often teach short introductory courses on the most popular software packages.

The time you spend learning about software capabilities will help simplify your PC hardware decisions. Your choice of software may affect how much PC memory you need, the type of disk drives you use, whether or not you need a color monitor, and the type of PC peripherals you need to do your tasks. Remember, a PC is simply a collection of hardware that runs software.

PC Operating Environments

The application software you choose also affects which PC operating environment you will be using. A PC operating environment is like a type of glue that binds the hardware and software together. An *operating environment* is a program that determines how you will operate application programs on your PC.

The PC Disk Operating System (DOS)

The most widely used PC operating environment is called DOS (disk operating system). When you start up a PC that uses only DOS as the operating environment, DOS performs all the housekeeping tasks required to get the computer going. DOS then waits for you to enter commands to tell it which application programs to run.

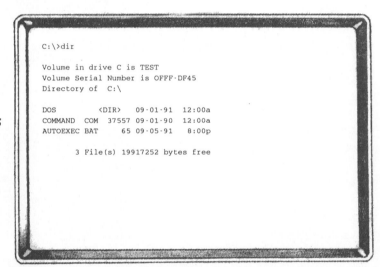

```
C:\>dir

Volume in drive C is TEST
Volume Serial Number is OFFF-DF45
Directory of  C:\

DOS          <DIR>   09-01-91  12:00a
COMMAND  COM 37557  09-01-90  12:00a
AUTOEXEC BAT    65  09-05-91   8:00p

        3 File(s) 19917252 bytes free
```

Typical DOS screen

DOS programs accept user commands that are typed on the keyboard. This form of user interface requires that the user be familiar with many DOS commands and how the commands are spelled. To make life easier, DOS can be run from within other programs called shells. A *shell* lets a user select DOS commands from lists, or *menus*. This way, users of shell programs do not have to memorize DOS commands. They simply learn to navigate the shell's menus to find and use commands.

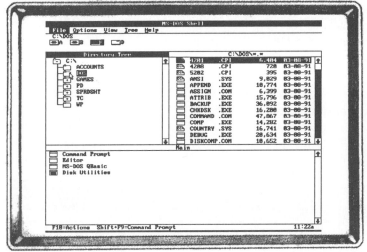

Example DOS
shell

Graphical User Interfaces (GUIs)

A *graphical user interface*, or *GUI* (pronounced "gooey"), is a type of operating environment that relies on a user's visual abilities. Objects on the screen are portrayed as small graphic symbols, called *icons*. You can select screen objects and menu items with a pointing device, such as a mouse or trackball.

GUI users are freer to concentrate on the tasks being performed. They do not have to memorize dozens of DOS commands and how those commands are spelled. In some GUI operating environments, users can open up a DOS window and access the DOS commands from that easy-to-use visual interface while running one or more application programs. Operating environments that let a user run more than one program at a time are called *multitasking environments*.

Generally, a DOS-type program costs less than a GUI. GUIs, however, offer the user easier PC command operations and multitasking capabilities. On PCs, GUIs come in two forms: low-end, low-cost programs that run on most PCs in nearly any PC hardware configuration, and high-end, high-cost programs that run only on the more powerful, more expensive PCs.

Good examples of low-end GUIs are DeskMate and GeoWorks. These GUIs provide low-cost operating environments that run on most PCs. In addition, they provide an integrated set of application programs that run addition, they provide an integrated set of application programs that run within the GUI's framework. For example, DeskMate comes with a collection of 20 programs to help you operate your PC, write letters, create databases, perform calculations, draw images, and communicate with other computers. GeoWorks and its companion package, GeoWorks Ensemble, provide both a state-of-the-art GUI and an integrated set of PC application programs.

The most widely used high-end GUI is Windows. Windows is an interface that lets you operate application programs expressly designed to run under Windows.

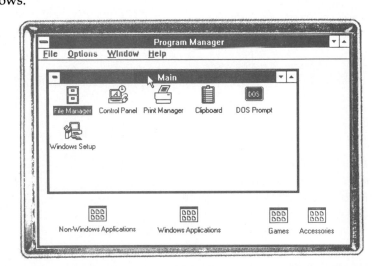

*Windows
screen*

Windows works best on a PC with lots of memory, a large, fast hard disk, and a powerful CPU. Windows comes bundled with a limited starter set of application programs. Additional application programs for Windows, and Windows itself, cost more than the low-end GUI counterparts.

Suggestions for Beginning PC Users

Gather as much information as possible before making final purchasing decisions. Acquire demonstration disks of the packages you might use.

Attend hands-on classes that show you what particular software packages do. Ask people who use computers to give you information and advice. Talk to neighbors, business colleagues, and teachers. Visit local computer stores. Ask salespeople to demonstrate products. Ask them about PC user groups in your area. Contact those groups and ask about presentations of the packages you are investigating.

To start, you may not want to buy the most expensive software. Some low-cost packages perform well and will meet your immediate needs. Many lower-priced packages are also easier to learn to use. You may wish to start small and upgrade to more complex, often more expensive, products as your needs increase. If possible, choose programs that your friends and coworkers already use. Ask them for advice and help in learning to use the programs you select.

Beginning PC users may want to start with a low-end, low-cost GUI such as DeskMate or GeoWorks. This will give you an opportunity to learn how a GUI works and also acquire a full range of low-cost integrated application programs. Later, once you have gained experience with your PC, you can look at upgrading your system and software. Many times, a low-end GUI and its application programs are all you will ever need.

Another way to acquire software products that you can "try before you buy" is with shareware products. *Shareware* is a software distribution concept. It enables software authors to provide copies of their products at little or no charge. You can try out a product, and if it seems to meet your needs, you send a registration fee directly to the authors. In return, you receive complete documentation, as well as technical support for any problems you encounter in using the product.

Shareware resources

One resource for shareware products and information is *Shareware* magazine. This magazine is published by PC-SIG, 1030D East Duane Ave., Sunnyvale, CA 94086. PC-SIG is a shareware distributor and provides access to over 2500 low-cost shareware programs. User groups are also good sources of shareware and public domain (free) programs. Visit your local computer store and ask about user groups.

File　Edit　Display

Report

File　Edit　Graph

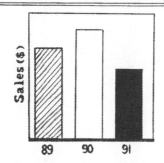

Sales ($)

89　90　91

File　Edit　Style　Graph

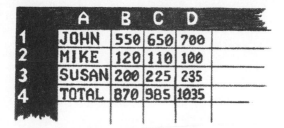

	A	B	C	D
1	JOHN	550	650	700
2	MIKE	120	110	100
3	SUSAN	200	225	235
4	TOTAL	870	985	1035

PC Productivity Software

4

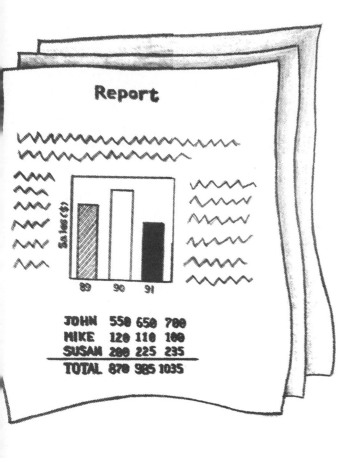

Report

JOHN 550 650 700
MIKE 120 110 100
SUSAN 200 225 235
TOTAL 870 985 1035

PC *productivity software* includes programs to help you create and edit documents, perform calculations, maintain lists of information, manage projects, and remind you of appointments. The three most commonly used programs for everyday productivity tasks, both in business and at home, are writing and editing packages, financial packages, and database management systems. Everyone who creates documents, performs financial calculations, or manages lists of data can benefit by using a PC and one or more productivity programs.

Writing and Editing Packages

The primary writing and editing program used on most PCs is a word processor. Word processors let you use a PC to type and edit documents ranging from a single page to an entire book. Word processors let you correct typing mistakes without having to retype an entire page or document. With a word processor, you can insert, delete, and move blocks of text in an instant. Many word processors help correct misspellings, give you control of the format and style of documents, and let you choose the appearance of the printed information. Some word processors come with an electronic thesaurus and dictionary that help you find the precise words you want to use.

Example word processor screen

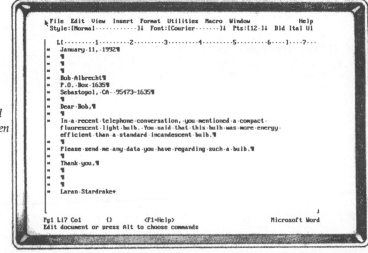

When you use a word processor, what you type appears on the monitor. You can then edit and make corrections directly on the screen. You can use a word processor to instantly change margin settings, line spacing, and tab controls. Some word processors also let you select the typefaces, or *fonts*, you wish to use, and the size and style of the fonts. If you want a word to appear in **bold** or *italic* letters, some PC word processors show you how that looks right on your screen.

Edit	View	Text	Style

Font...
Alignment
Indention...
Spacing...

Normal
Bold
Italic
Underline

One major difference between a word processor and a typewriter is a feature called *word wrap*. On a typewriter, each time you reach the end of line, you have to press the RETURN key to advance the carriage to a new line. On a PC with a word processor, the program automatically shifts to a new line each time you exceed the available space on the current line. If needed, the program moves the partial word you are typing down to the new line as well.

The best part of the word-wrap feature involves more than eliminating Return keys. If your PC word processor has a word-wrap feature, when you insert text into the middle of a paragraph, the entire bottom half of the paragraph is adjusted instantly to accommodate all of the new text. To insert new text on a typewriter, you would have to retype the entire paragraph, perhaps the entire page, and possibly the complete document.

With a word processor, you seldom have to retype any text that you have already entered into the PC. Also, you can "cut and paste" text electronically, moving blocks of text to new locations within a document or even between documents and different programs.

File	Edit	Display	Font

Undo   ^U

Cut
Copy
Paste

Copy To...
Paste From...

Typical edit menu options

Other Writing and Editing Program Features

In addition to the many standard features already mentioned (format controls, font controls, word wrap, and so forth), PC word processors may also support additional features. For example, some programs help you create and manipulate outlines that assist you in structuring your documents. Some programs let you specify and create tables and multicolumn text entries. Still others let you include graphics images as part of the document.

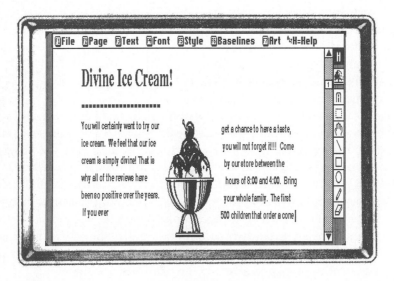

Document with text and graphics

There are writing and editing programs that correct grammar, create alphabetized indexes of words along with the page numbers where the words occur, and manage footnotes and bibliographies. There are specialized word processors available for writing television and movie scripts, novels, and poetry. There are word processors that help you come up with new ideas and concepts.

Before settling on any one word processing package, carefully review your needs for such a package. Then, look for the writing and editing system that most closely matches the tasks you plan to do with your PC.

Popular PC Word Processors

The two most widely used high-end PC word processing programs are WordPerfect and Microsoft Word. Used mostly by professionals, these products are state-of-the-art word processors. Many thousands of PC users still word process documents using WordStar, one of the original PC word processing packages. WordStar has recently been upgraded so it can better compete with the two leaders.

These leading packages, designed for heavy-duty document-creation tasks, have steep learning curves. Except for special-purpose word processors designed exclusively for professional writers, these packages are also the most expensive. Mid-range and low-end word processing products exist that are easier to use and cost less. Professional Write is a mid-range product in terms of both features and costs. PFS: First Choice contains a word processor in its set of low-cost integrated programs. Microsoft Works is another set of popular integrated programs that includes a word processor.

Beginning PC users are encouraged to look at inexpensive word processors before making final choices. Explore programs like the popular, full-featured shareware products PC-Write and Galaxy Lite. Also, investigate the word processors that come with low-cost GUIs such as DeskMate and GeoWorks.

Financial Packages

PCs are good at doing calculations, or *number crunching*. Most computers were originally designed to assist with tedious computation tasks involving many numbers and numerical operations.

One type of calculation program that actually helped launch the PC revolution is the electronic spreadsheet. Where a word processor helps you process letters, words, sentences, and paragraphs, a spreadsheet helps you process numbers and relationships between numbers.

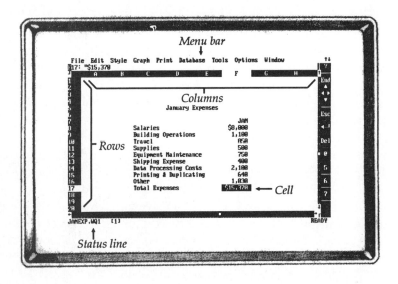

Example spreadsheet display

Electronic spreadsheets were designed to replace the paper ledger sheets used by bookkeepers and accountants. Putting the sheet on a computer screen, with hundreds of row and column positions, or *cells*, gave planners and financial analysts a tool that let them quickly and easily customize calculations to fit particular business and financial needs. Tedious, error-prone hand computations gave way to instantaneous, error-free results. In addition, spreadsheet users discovered that they could easily change numbers or relationships and recalculate answers with the push of a key.

The great success of electronic spreadsheets, still the most popular type of financial program, has influenced the creation of a number of special-purpose financial packages for both home and business. Today you will find PC financial packages that help you manage your checkbook, plan and

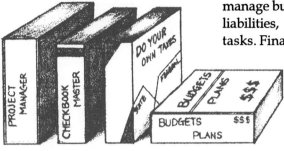

manage budgets, manage assets and liabilities, and perform accounting tasks. Financial programs exist that help you prepare your annual tax information and manage and analyze personal and business projects.

Special Features in Financial Packages

Beyond performing computations, some financial packages also help you assemble and graph information. If you need to both analyze and present results from your financial calculations, you may want to look at packages that have complete charting and graphing capabilities.

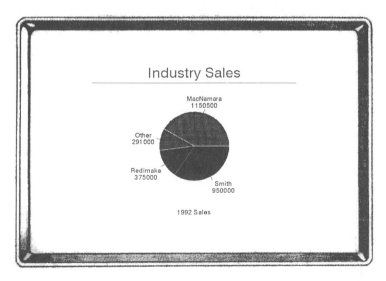

Spreadsheet graph and chart features

If you need to work with large amounts of data, you may wish to consider one of the more advanced financial packages. These packages combine several functions, such as an electronic spreadsheet, a database, and a graphics display capability into a single program. These packages are more complex to use. But, when managing large amounts of data and financial relationships, you may need such a package to efficiently perform your required tasks.

Popular PC Spreadsheet Packages

Three of the most popular PC spreadsheet programs are Lotus 1-2-3, Microsoft Excel, and Quattro Pro. Lotus 1-2-3 is an integrated package that includes an electronic spreadsheet, a database, and a graphics program. Excel was designed to run under Windows, the high-end PC GUI. Quattro Pro is a slightly lower cost spreadsheet program that is compatible with Lotus 1-2-3.

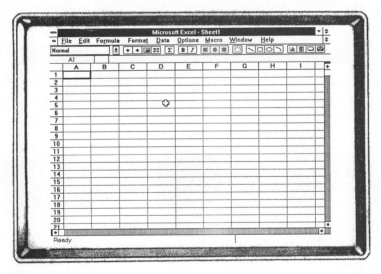

Excel spreadsheet display

Again, beginning PC users are advised to look into low-cost and integrated-program spreadsheet options. PC-Calc+, a shareware product, is an inexpensive way to get access to a powerful spreadsheet. PFS: First Choice also supports a low-cost integrated spreadsheet, as do the low-end GUIs DeskMate and GeoWorks. Microsoft Works contains an integrated spreadsheet program. Lotus 1-2-3 comes in many different versions, including a simplified, less expensive product that runs under DeskMate.

Database Management Systems (DBMS)

A database management system helps you create, edit, sort, retrieve, and print collections of electronic information, called databases. A *database* is any collection of information that has been organized and stored in some meaningful way.

For example, you might keep a large list of the names and addresses of everyone you know. Some of these people might be business associates, members of your tennis club, people you know who enjoy sailing, members of your glee club, and so forth. A PC and a database program can help you organize this list so you can quickly locate any business associates who like to sail or any tennis club members who are also in your folk dance club.

A database program not only lets you search and retrieve selected information, it also helps you print and display that data. For example, you may want to send out an announcement of an event at your local harbor to glee club members who like to sail. Once you have retrieved the names and addresses of glee club people who like to sail, you can use a database program to print a set of mailing labels for those people.

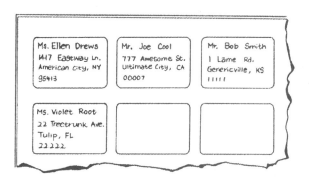

Database programs, when coupled with a word processor, can help you create form letters. *Form letters* are documents that contain virtually the same information except for one or two items like the recipient's name and address. With a database program, you can extract the needed names and addresses and merge those items into copies of the document as they are printed by the word processor.

What to Look for in a DBMS

Every DBMS performs at least the following procedures:

- Data entry and editing
- Data retrieval
- Sorting
- Printing and Reporting

The data entry and editing part of the DBMS is a key program element. It either simplifies or complicates your database creation tasks, as well as the entry and editing of data. Most recent database programs let you create databases using sets of visual tools. With these tools, you can create and edit the structure of your database directly on the screen.

Automotive Maintenance and Repair Records

DBMS form that can be edited on the screen

Flexible database packages let you retrieve and sort data using criteria that you determine. Many older database systems restrict the number of search and sort parameters that can be used. Attempts to extract data from a database with limited features may result in more work on your part to retrieve the data you wish to see.

Finally, the DBMS you choose should have flexible print and report capabilities. Check to see if the program you are considering produces mailing labels, form letters, and easy-to-define customized reports. Verify that the program will print to the printer you already have or plan to use.

Before purchasing a DBMS package, make sure you know what type of data files you plan to create. Also, try to determine now how big your database is likely to get in the future. Databases always have a tendency to grow larger than expected. The ultimate size of a database affects the performance of the chosen software package, the size and speed of disk drives you will need, and the amount of computing power that is needed in your PC.

Popular DBMS Packages

The first major database program for the PC, called dBASE, created hordes of advocates and nearly as many skeptics. Early versions of dBASE required programming skills beyond the reach of most beginning users. Recent versions have simplified many of dBASE's original complexities. Newer DBMS entries include Paradox, Q&A, and FoxPro. Q&A is an integrated set of programs that includes a database program, a word processor, and a report generator. Q&A lets users query the database by using "natural language" commands. For example, users can ask the database program to "find names of all people in the folk dance club."

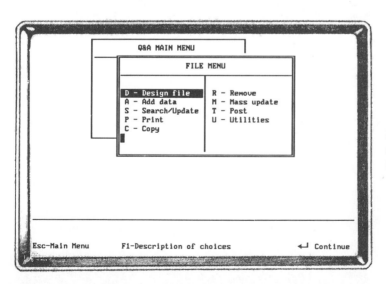

Example screen from Q&A DBMS

For low-cost DBMS options, beginning users might try the shareware product, PC-FILE. PC-FILE comes with extensive report and charting features. Low-end GUIs, such as DeskMate and GeoWorks, have integrated DBMS capabilities. Integrated products like PFS: First Choice and Microsoft Works also support DBMS features.

Integrated Software Packages

If you think you need a word processor, a spreadsheet program, and a database management system, be sure to examine one or more of the PC integrated software packages. As the name implies, an integrated software package includes several software programs in a single package.

Word Processing

Spreadsheet

Communications

Database

Typical integrated package features

There are many advantages, especially for beginners, in selecting an integrated package over several different pieces of software. One advantage is that data created in one part of an integrated package can be used in another part, automatically. You can transfer data from the database into the word processor, from the word processor into the spreadsheet, and from the spreadsheet into the database—in other words, from any application to any other application.

A second advantage is that when you learn how to use one part of an integrated package, you often learn the mechanics of operating the other parts as well. Good integrated packages keep the user interface simple and as consistent as possible among all parts of the package.

A third advantage is that you will probably pay less for an integrated package than you would for several different programs. This is true particularly if you decide that you can use an integrated package like DeskMate. DeskMate, a low-cost GUI, comes with a word processor, database program, graphics program, spreadsheet, and communications programs as standard features of the user interface. GeoWorks, another low-cost GUI, has a package of integrated products, called GeoWorks Ensemble, which is sold separately.

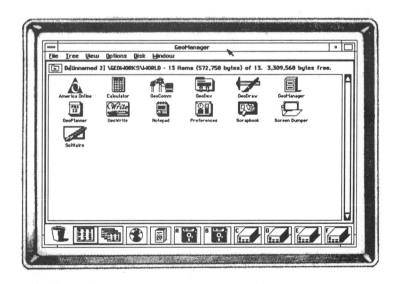

GeoWorks Ensemble display

PFS: First Choice includes a word processor, spreadsheet, database program, graphics features, and a communications program. Microsoft Works has the same features as PFS: First Choice minus the graphics features. Enable/OA is a more costly and more sophis-

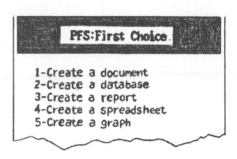

ticated integrated package. Enable/OA, like many integrated packages, lets you use more than one program feature at the same time and lets you switch easily between applications.

Tips for Selecting a PC Productivity Package

To start, determine your needs for PC productivity software capabilities. Do you need a writing and editing system? Do you need a spreadsheet? Will you be managing lots of data with your PC? Will you be doing all three of these things? Then, ask your friends and coworkers about the programs they use for productivity tasks. Locate and read product reviews and comparisons in PC magazines. Check to see if an integrated package or a low-cost GUI meets your needs. If possible, get hands-on experience with the packages you are considering before making a final decision.

Graphics and Desktop Publishing on the PC

5

Colorful PC graphics images first appeared in computer games. Since then, the demand for more and better PC graphics has escalated. Now, PC users can buy graphics programs that create sophisticated, colorful images, including moving images (animations) and renderings of solid objects (3-D images). Advances in PC graphics programs have led to the creation of word processors that accept graphics images. PC users can now mix text and graphics on the same screen.

These breakthroughs fostered the development of PC *desktop publishing (DTP)* packages. DTP programs let you perform every step in publishing a document: text entry, typesetting, creation and insertion of images, layout, and printing.

Taken together, graphics programs and DTP packages have changed how graphic artists, designers, writers, typesetters, and publishers do their jobs. You can use many of these programs to produce newsletters, flyers, greeting cards, and personal computer art.

Graphics Programs

PC graphics programs fall into three general categories: paint programs, draw programs, and a set of sophisticated computer-aided design (CAD) packages. *Paint programs* let a PC user "paint" and edit images directly on

Example paint program display

the screen. Paint programs come with sets of tools, brushes, textures, colors, and shapes to assist in making PC graphics images.

Draw programs let users assemble images from sets of graphics objects. Each graphics *object*, or part of an image, is created separately. You form final images combining one or more objects. Draw program images are used in situations in which you require more sophisticated graphics and higher quality printed images than you can achieve with paint programs.

Typical draw program display

CAD programs produce the highest quality, most sophisticated PC graphics images. CAD programs are used by architects, engineers, designers, and graphic artists to produce images of buildings, cars, computer circuits, animated cartoons, and TV commercials.

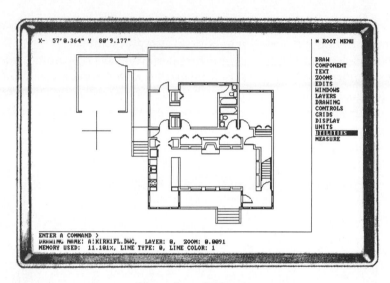

View using a CAD system

Paint Programs

There are many modestly priced, powerful PC paint programs. Examples include Dr. Halo III, PC Paintbrush, Paintshow Plus, and Deluxe Paint.

Low-cost GUIs and integrated product sets often contain excellent graphics programs. Some graphics programs, such as Paintshow Plus, let you display collections of graphics images in the form of a slide show.

You can acquire disks full of predrawn images, called *clip art*. With a paint program, you can load and edit clip-art images and use the graphics in

Sample clip art

your PC-generated newsletters, flyers, slideshows, and greeting cards. PC paint programs and clip art give everyone an opportunity to express themselves on the PC.

To use any graphics program effectively, you need a pointing device on your PC. Pen and stylus systems, although more costly, work best. With them, you feel like you are painting or drawing with a brush or pencil. Using a mouse or trackball requires effort, practice, and patience. If you plan on producing professional graphics images or simply want to draw more easily, investigate pen and stylus systems. Before making a final choice, verify that the graphics programs you select supports the pointing device you wish to use.

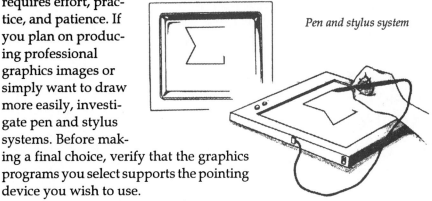

Pen and stylus system

If you plan on drawing color images, your PC system will have to have a color monitor. Most home users do not need the same quality monitors as professional PC users. Professional PC artists need more expensive, higher resolution color monitors.

Draw Programs

PC draw programs were designed to give PC users greater control over the production and printing of graphics images. Consequently, draw programs often support more tools and features than paint programs. Draw programs are slightly more complex to use but let you produce professional PC graphics images.

The graphics programs in DeskMate and GeoWorks Ensemble, the low-end GUIs, are both draw-style programs. Beginning PC owners can use these programs to learn the basics of operating a draw program. Some users may find these draw applications powerful enough for many of their graphics production needs.

High-end, professional draw programs include Corel Draw, Adobe Illustrator, Micrografx Designer, and DrawPerfect. These programs, designed for high-quality graphics production tasks, are expensive to purchase and maintain. For beginners, start with a low-cost program and upgrade to a high-end, expensive draw package as your skills and needs increase.

If you reach a point where you think you need a professional draw package, do some research. Talk with people who are using the various products. Look at product demonstrations at local computer stores. If possible, take classes where you actually use the products. Also, look through PC magazines for articles that compare the features and shortcomings of the various packages.

CAD Programs

CAD programs provide sophisticated PC tools for producing 3-D drawings, animated images, schematics, architectural plans, and engineering designs. Prices for CAD programs range from under a hundred dollars to several thousand dollars.

Popular PC CAD programs include AutoCAD, Generic CADD, Easy CAD, AutoSketch, Design CAD, Turbo CAD, and CCS Designer. Few PC users will ever need to use a sophisticated CAD program.

Desktop Publishing (DTP) Packages

DTP packages let you use the PC and a printer as a complete publishing tool. If you want to use the PC to help you publish a newsletter, occasional flyers, brochures and pamphlets, proposals, reports, or any type of professional-looking document, DTP programs are the way to go.

DTP packages let you design your documents on the screen. You can rely on the DTP programs' WYSIWYG (What You See Is What You Get—"wizzy-wig") features to help you visualize and assemble electronic pages. With a DTP program, you write and edit your text in your favorite word processor, draw or paint images by using your favorite graphics programs, and then assemble everything by using the DTP package.

Desktop publishing package with WYSIWYG display

The success of DTP programs has prompted word processor developers to include some DTP features in their programs. Many word processors now have extended printer and font capabilities, as well as some page layout features. DTP program developers, on the other hand, have been adding more word processing features to their packages. Many DTP programs now spell-check text, provide thesaurus and dictionary features, and let users edit both graphics and text. In the future, all word processors and integrated product sets may include full DTP capabilities.

Low-end and Mid-range DTP Packages

Several good DTP packages are available in a low to middle range of prices and capabilities. Here are the names of a few such programs: Publish It!, Express Publisher, PFS: First Publisher, and Finesse DTP.

These packages may not provide all the features of the high-end DTP programs (discussed in the following section). The packages generally provide easy-to-use products that work in many home and small business situations. If you plan to publish large documents, documents with complex page layout requirements, or documents that must meet professional scrutiny, investigate the high-end DTP packages or services.

High-end DTP Packages

The majority of high-end DTP production work is done by using one of these PC packages: PageMaker or Ventura Publisher. These programs let you use text created in any of several word processors and import graphics from a variety of graphics programs and clip-art libraries. They support extensive font capabilities and on-screen graphical elements such as rules, boxes, and shaded backgrounds.

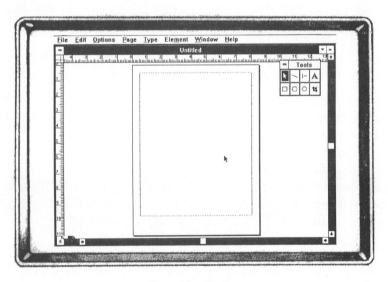

PageMaker display

A beginning PC user is unlikely to need the publishing power of a high-end DTP package right away. With experience both on the PC and with low-end or mid-range DTP products, that same user may one day require the power of PageMaker or Ventura Publisher. If that requirement is merely a one-time need, users may want to hire a DTP service to take the document to final form.

DTP service organizations evolved out of the convenience centers that rent time on computers. Because high-end DTP packages are difficult to learn to use, many such centers find that people are willing to buy design and DTP services. Confronted with a complex DTP product, you may think it more efficient to let the center's DTP experts do the job. If you make that choice, sit with the expert as he or she assembles and lays out your document. You will learn a great deal about the DTP packages being used.

Other Types of PC Software

Other types of PC software include education, entertainment, communications, and utilities programs.

Education Programs

Some of the best PC education, or learning, programs are also great entertainment software. The Carmen Sandiego product series provides hours of fun-filled, information-packed, problem-solving adventures for the whole family. For younger children, there is the colorful Super Solver series and The Playroom. Do you want to learn to type? Mavis Beacon Teaches Typing has been a top-selling PC education program for some time.

Shareware's answer to Mavis Beacon is PC Fast Type. Another amusing shareware product is Googol Math Games. Do you want to build cities and run an entire planet? Look into SimCity and SimEarth, two popular PC simulation/learning products. There are hundreds of other PC education programs to help you learn just about any-

Scene from The Playroom

thing. You can use the PC to learn how to read, learn a language, study math and science, explore history, and even discover how to use your PC.

Two of the best resources for information about PC learning products are friends and teachers. Ask them about their favorite programs. How are the

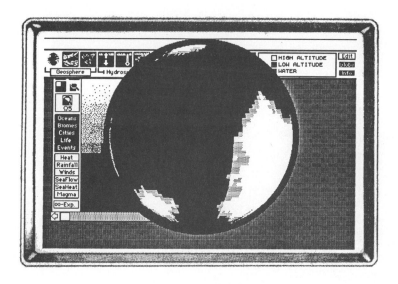

The SimEarth program

programs used in the home and in school? Will the PC need any special hardware? Remember, most good PC educational programs are best seen in color on a color monitor. Also, a few packages require special hardware boards for speech and sound production. Most education and entertainment programs work better with a pointing device such as a mouse or trackball.

Entertainment Programs

PC entertainment software comes in a variety of formats. There are fast-paced arcade games, fantasy role-playing games, strategy games, puzzles, and simulations. You can also use the PC to play chess, cards, and nearly every popular board game. Simulations, especially flight simulators, continue to be a popular type of PC entertainment program. If you have a secret desire to fly a supersonic jet or drive in high-speed races, check out one of the many PC simulators now available.

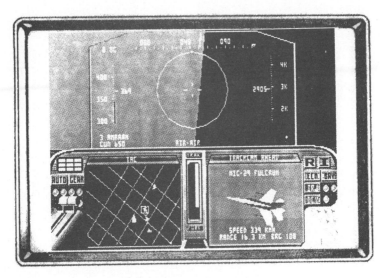

Typical flight simulator screen

In the fantasy role-playing arena, the King's Quest series is a proven entertainment product. A good fantasy role-playing shareware product is Commander Keen. Recent arcade-style puzzles, such as Tetris and its shareware counterpart, Nyet, are enjoyed by kids of all ages. *Computer Gaming World*, a magazine dedicated to computer strategy, simulation,

Scenes from King's Quest game

role-playing adventure, arcade, and war games, maintains a monthly list of the top 100 reader-selected games. Check with your friends who have PCs. Ask them to let you play their favorite PC games and entertainment products.

To get the most enjoyment out of current PC entertainment packages, your PC will need a color monitor and a pointing device. In the future, PC entertainment programs will be distributed on a type of high-density medium like a CD (compact disc). The immense storage capacity of this type of disk will provide video quality, moving images along with high-quality stereo sound tracks. To enjoy these future PC entertainment programs, your PC will have to have a CD hardware unit in addition to its regular disk drives.

Communications Programs

PC communications programs turn your PC into a data sending and receiving station. If two PCs are in the same room or building, they can exchange information over a cable. If the PCs are across town or in another city, they need to be connected by modems and telephone lines. A modem is a hardware device that translates and decodes computer information being sent over telephone lines. For long-distance communications, both PCs require a modem and a PC communications program.

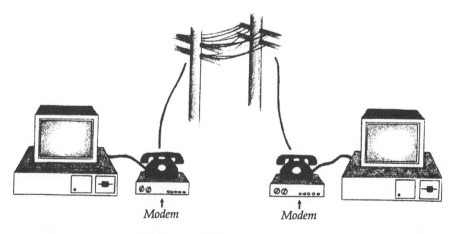

Modem   *Modem*

Communications between two remote PCs

A few communications programs, such as LapLink, come with a cable that lets you link two PCs and exchange information directly. Versions of LapLink even let you exchange data files between PCs and other types of computers. Communications programs that let you link two remote PCs over modems include popular products such as ProComm Plus, SmartCom, and CrossTalk.

```
                        P r o C o m m   H e l p

     MAJOR FUNCTIONS          UTILITY FUNCTIONS          FILE FUNCTIONS

Dialing Directory . Alt-D   Program Info ...... Alt-I   Send files ....... PgUp
Automatic Redial... Alt-R   Setup Screen ...... Alt-S   Receive files ... PgDn
Keyboard Macros ... Alt-M   Kermit Server Cmd . Alt-K   Directory ...... Alt-F
Line Settings ..... Alt-P   Change Directory .. Alt-B   View a File .... Alt-V
Translate Table ... Alt-W   Clear Screen ...... Alt-C   Screen Dump .... Alt-G
Editor ............ Alt-W   Toggle Duplex ..... Alt-E   Log Toggle .... Alt-F1
Exit .............. Alt-X   Hang Up Phone ..... Alt-H   Log Hold ...... Alt-F2
Host Mode ......... Alt-Q   Elapsed Time ...... Alt-T
Chat Mode ......... Alt-O   Print On/Off ...... Alt-L
DOS Gateway ...... Alt-F4   Set Colors ........ Alt-Z
Command Files .... Alt-F5   Auto Answer ....... Alt-Y
Redisplay ........ Alt-F6   Toggle CR-CR/LF .. Alt-F3
                            Break Key ........ Alt-F7

                    Datastorm Technologies, Inc.
```

ProComm telecommunications software

Many integrated products, such as PFS: First Choice and Microsoft Works, also include communications programs. The low-end GUIs, Desk-Mate and GeoWorks, offer communications programs as part of the standard interface applications. Shareware communications programs are some of the best in the industry. Many shareware communications products, such as Telix, offer all the features of commercial packages at a much lower cost. An earlier version of ProComm Plus was first introduced as a shareware product.

A PC, modem, and communications program let you access a new world of electronic information. You can go online to any number of *information services*, such as CompuServe, Prodigy, PC Link, Dow Jones, DIALOG, Delphi, MCI Mail, and GEnie. You can also access any of thousands of electronic *bulletin board systems (BBS)*. On these services and systems, you can send mail, browse through information, have electronic discussions, join user groups, play games, download programs into your PC, and meet mysterious electronic friends.

Recent innovations in hardware technologies let you turn your PC into a complete home office communications station. You can now buy modems that include fax (facsimile) and voice mail options. Some of these units let you do several tasks concurrently. As you prepare an electronic letter to a friend, your PC can be sending or receiving a fax transmission or recording an electronic voice message from your personal telephone.

Utility Programs

PC utility programs help you manage and use your PC more effectively. Some programs, such as PC Tools Deluxe and Norton Utilities, assist you with organizing, optimizing, and maintaining your disk drives and files. Other packages, such as HiJaak and InSet, help you capture, manipulate, and transfer graphics images between various programs and computers.

Norton Utilities program

Utility programs exist that let you produce higher quality images on your printer and that speed up your PC's operations. There are PC *desk accessory* or *memory-resident programs*, like SideKick, that you load and use while running other applications. These types of utilities help you take notes, manage personal schedules, maintain address book files, and provide a variety of on-screen electronic calculators, and they can even dial telephone numbers for you.

The type and number of utility programs on anyone's PC is a matter of personal needs and preferences. Utility programs let you customize to your requirements the way your PC works. For example, there are utility programs that let you record often-used keystroke sequences and replay those sequences with the touch of a single key. In this way, you can organize repetitive tasks into a collection of single-key operations that only you understand and know.

The best sources of information about utility programs are your friends with PCs and PC user groups. Also, watch the PC magazines for articles that compare the features and benefits of various PC utilities. With utility programs, start slowly and add programs as your personal computing needs develop.

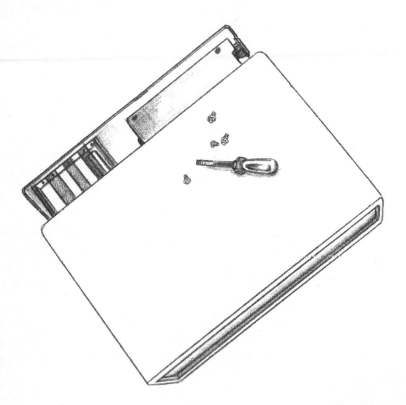

Important PC Hardware Information

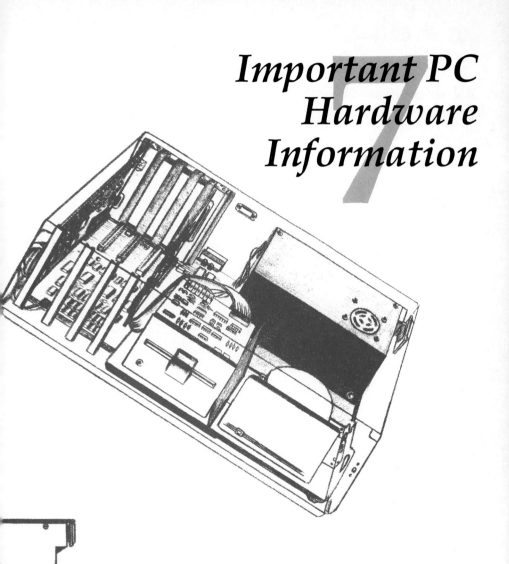

To make an informed selection of a PC hardware system, you need to know the following:

- What tasks you wish to perform on your PC and what types of software programs will help you with those tasks

- Basic information about PC hardware components and terminology

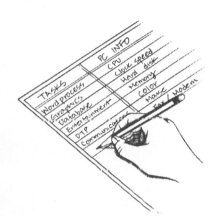

The earlier parts of this book discussed the types of PC software you might look at as you think about the tasks you plan to do. You were encouraged to talk with friends, visit computer stores, read PC and consumer magazines, contact user groups, and most important, try to get hands-on experience with the products you might like to use.

The next few chapters of this book give you an introduction to PC hardware terminology and additional specifics about the hardware itself. The goal is to provide you with enough information and familiarity about PC hardware to make you comfortable with the PC system you have or plan to acquire. When you complete the remainder of this book, you will be able to discuss and decode the handful of PC technical concepts that influence the type of PC system you need to accomplish your tasks. You will be able to do so with confidence.

Understanding PC Terminology

Your first encounter with PC terminology occurs when you look at advertisements for PC systems. You see mysterious listings for PC systems that look like the following:

YURPC 286/12, 512KB (exp. 2 MB), 42MB, Mono $775

When you first look at such hieroglyphics, only one obvious fact seems clear—the larger the numbers, the more everything costs.

Deciphering PC Advertising Shorthand

Advertisements for PCs have been turned into a type of shorthand notation. One reason for this is the huge number of options you can exercise when acquiring a PC system.

The options have been standardized and reduced to a series of codes that succinctly, but mysteriously, describe what is being offered. Breaking the code is not that difficult.

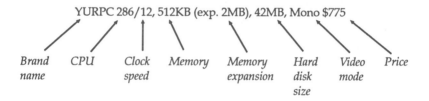

In the listings, the first item (YURPC in the example) represents the brand name of the computer. Some major brand names are more recognizable than others (IBM, Tandy, Compaq, and so forth). Dozens of other PC brand names have emerged as manufacturers and have built PC systems to compete with the major brands.

The next item in the listing (286/12) is shorthand for the type of microprocessor chip being used (286) and how fast the chip can operate (12). The chip is the Intel 80286 microprocessor. It runs at a clock speed of 12 megahertz (MHz). A *hertz* is one clock tick per second. A *megahertz* is one million clock ticks per second. This CPU operates at 12 million clock ticks per second!

In general, the more power a chip has, the larger its CPU number (286, 386, 486). A chip's speed increases as the megahertz (MHz) number increases (12, 25, 33, and so forth).

A Brief Look at Microprocessors

The microprocessor chip (or CPU) is like the engine in your car. You can have a four-cylinder engine, a six-cylinder engine, or an eight-cylinder engine. In general, the bigger the engine, the more horsepower you have under the hood.

The same is roughly true for microprocessors. Early CPUs (with chip names such as 8088 and 8086) are now like four-cylinder antique cars. They did the job but were not very powerful. A few of these antique systems are still being marketed, but no one should consider getting a PC with one of these older CPUs.

PCs with 286 and 386SX CPUs are like today's more modern four-cylinder automobiles. PCs with 386DX and 386 chips with high clock speeds (386/25, 386/33, and so forth) can be likened to sturdy six-cylinder cars, while computers with 486 chips can be compared to cars with the biggest engines.

The SX and DX notations identify two classes of Intel 80386 chips. The 386SX is a scaled-down, less powerful version of the 386DX chip. In this

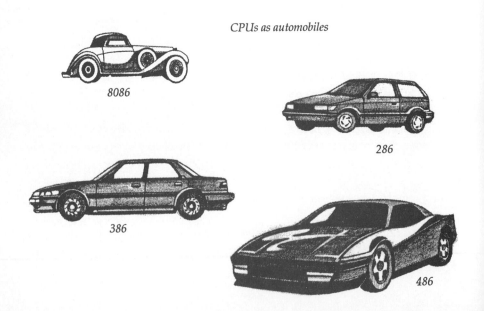

CPUs as automobiles

8086

286

386

486

book, and in most PC advertisements, any reference to a plain "386" CPU means that the system is using a 386DX or equivalent microprocessor.

The different types of CPUs in today's PCs tend to have clock speeds that fall within a range of MHz values. The combination of the engine (the CPU) and the clock speed determines how much power you have under your PC hood. To perform well on most of today's software, a PC with a 286 chip needs a clock speed between 12 and 16 MHz. A PC with a 386SX CPU operates somewhere between 16 and 25 MHz. PCs using 386DX chips have clock speeds ranging from 16 to 33 MHz. Clock speeds for today's 486 chips fall between 25 and 33 MHz, and there are rumors of higher clock speeds becoming available for the 486.

As you investigate how much PC power you will need, try running any software you plan to acquire on different PCs. Notice the performance variations as you try a range of systems, chips, and clock speeds. Ultimately, you will have to

CPU	Clock Speed					
	12	16	20	25	33	50
286	✓	✓				
386 SX		✓	✓	✓		
386		✓	✓	✓	✓	
486				✓	✓	✓

CPU/speed matrix with checked off entries

balance the size of your pocketbook against your desire for speed and convenience. Looking at a range of options will help you choose a PC system that fits your needs.

Memory, Disk Drives, and Video Capabilities

Now you know the brand name of the PC (YURPC), the type of CPU (286), and the chip's clock speed (12). The next part of the coded advertisement tells you how much memory the PC comes with (512KB, or 512 kilobytes). One kilobyte is equal to 1024 bytes, or characters. This system has 512 kilobytes (512x1024 bytes), or 524,288 bytes of memory. This amount of memory is not enough to efficiently run much of today's best software.

The listing indicates that this PC's memory capacity can be expanded (exp. 2MB) up to 2 megabytes (2,097,152 bytes). You need at least one megabyte (1MB) of memory to run today's best software. Of course, you have to pay more to get additional memory. A PC with 1MB has more than enough memory to run low-cost GUIs such as DeskMate and GeoWorks. To run Windows on a low-powered PC like this 286/12 system, you need a full 2MB of memory. Even so, you still may not like how slowly Windows performs on this type of system.

The advertised system comes with a hard disk, denoted by the code 42MB. You can distinguish numbers designating memory size from hard disk codes by the magnitude of the entries. For example, memory numbers normally range from 512KB up to 8MB or more. Hard disk capacities start around 20MB and range up into the hundreds of millions of bytes.

The final two items in the listing tell you what type of video output the system provides (mono, or monochrome) and the price of the unit. Note that the listed price may or may not include the cost of a monitor. You have to look carefully at the fine print in and around the advertisements to learn what is and is not included in the listed price.

Batteries Included and Other Options

The fine print in advertisements and product specifications tell you what you get in the basic price and what you purchase as a set of options. For example, items commonly included in the listed price are the following:

- Choice of floppy disk drive
- Various ports for connecting external devices
- Keyboard
- Type of case or chassis
- Clock/calendar
- Hard disk/floppy disk controller
- Power supply
- Expansion slots
- Bundled software

Optional items are usually listed along with prices for such items. Options may include the following:

- A hard drive if no hard disk drive is included
- A monitor if no monitor is included
- An upgrade to a higher video resolution
- A mouse or other pointing device
- Memory expansion
- A printer
- A math coprocessor (like adding a turbo charger)
- Software (sometimes at discount prices)

The decision to add optional equipment is similar to that of buying a new car and looking at dealer options. Suppose the dealer offers a wonderful, but expensive, CD stereo system. You know where to get the same system at a better price if you do the installation. You can put off adding the option as long as you can handle the installation task. If you know nothing about installing car stereo systems, and you want a CD unit in your car, you may find it more cost effective to go with the dealer's package.

With needed PC options, look into similar hidden costs or pitfalls associated with adding options at a later date. For example, you may want to enhance your PC's music-making capabilities. To do so requires that you install a sound board in one of the PC's expansion slots inside the chassis. The task is not difficult, but if you are uncomfortable opening up your PC, you may ask the dealer to do the job.

Also, it pays to shop around for the entire PC system, including needed options, just as it often pays to shop around when buying a car. Different dealers offer a variety of specials, discounts, and incentives. They especially do so when they know a person is shopping comparatively at several locations.

But before you run out and use your newly acquired skills of decoding PC advertisements, read through Chapter 8, "Selecting PC Hardware Systems," which relates what you just learned about hardware terminology to what you already know about software. The result will be to give you a clear idea of how combinations of software and hardware systems can meet people's specific needs.

Selecting PC Hardware Systems

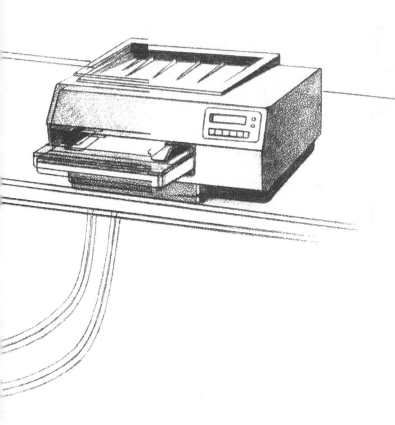

One way to organize information about selecting PC hardware systems is to imagine different types of users and what each one needs in order to do his or her tasks. Each type of user, such as a college student, a small business owner, an engineer, or a salesperson, has particular PC software and, consequently, hardware requirements.

This chapter outlines a set of likely PC users or situations and the types of hardware systems that might be needed. As you read through the descriptions, ask yourself how similar your needs are to those being presented. No one description is likely to match exactly what you need. But by the end of the chapter, you will have a good sense of where your needs fall within the range of the examples given.

All cost information in this chapter is addressed in a relative way. That is, systems and system components are characterized as being low , medium-, or high-cost, in relationship to each other. Because of rapid advances in technology, hardware costs will continue to fall, as they have since the introduction of computers. However, you can still anticipate that you will always see a range of PC prices and features in advertisements and product brochures. In general, you will find PCs grouped into three domains:

- Low-cost, low- to medium-powered PCs
- Middle-cost, middle- to high-powered computers
- High-cost, state-of-the-art technologies

The code numbers you reviewed in Chapter 7, "Important PC Hardware Information," may change over time. Just as newer microprocessors (286s, 386s, 486s) replaced older CPUs (8088s and 8086s), eventually these newer chips will give way to more powerful components. Despite these shifts and changes, you will still be able to make intelligent PC acquisition decisions based on what you learn in the remainder of this chapter.

A PC for a Thrifty Person

A thrifty individual might not be able to afford a GUI or other expensive software, and instead would probably plan to use DOS, which will run effectively on a lower cost, and probably slower, PC. A simple, low-cost database program, word processor, and spreadsheet would be sufficient to help with these tasks. When cost is a factor, it is a good idea to investigate several shareware products, because some have features that rival more expensive software packages. And someone not interested in fancy, laser-printed documents would be satisfied with a low-cost, relatively simple dot-matrix printer.

What type of hardware system should the economical person investigate? Providing he or she has no specific need for a really powerful PC, a low-cost PC system with a 286 CPU will do. Even if one must be really frugal, it is important not to get a PC with one of the older chips (8088 and 8086), because newer programs are optimized around the capabilities of the more modern chip sets. If the thrifty person is looking ahead, it may be more practical to buy a 80386 machine. Future software will probably require a 80386 chip, so a little money spent now may save a lot later on.

What about the clock speed on the PC? Well, you could get good performance out of a PC with a 286/12 chip, but a clock speed of 12MHz is about the slowest anyone would want to use. At speeds less than 12MHz, a computer will struggle to compute interest tables to the last penny.

A minimum PC system with the following specifications

CHEAP 286/12, 512KB (exp. 640 KB), Mono

might be a good choice.

In this example, the computer has the brand name CHEAP and has a low-speed 286 CPU (with a clock speed of 12MHz). The system comes with 512 kilobytes of memory (expandable to 640KB) and has monochrome video capacity. In this case, the CHEAP system comes with a small monochrome monitor.

This system does not have a hard disk drive. It does come with one built-in floppy disk drive, but operating a PC with a single floppy disk drive is awfully time-consuming. You spend most of your time removing and inserting disks as the PC labors to perform all of your tasks. Eventually, even a thrifty person may break down and buy a hard disk drive. With the addition of a 20MB hard drive, this inexpensive PC system can now be described as follows:

CHEAP 286/12, 512KB (exp. 640), 20 MB, Mono

A PC for a Student

A student might need a PC to capture research information and write term papers. More important, a student might need a system that is portable

in order to take it to classes and to the library or, perhaps, to the park to work on term papers. A good PC for a student might be a lightweight notebook computer with a hard disk that operates from batteries during the periods it is taken away from a desk. At a desk, a student can plug it into a wall outlet and use the computer while charging the batteries. For the typical student, color capabilities are unnecessary, but good screen resolution, especially for WYSIWYG text documents, is important. The description of this notebook PC might be as follows:

NoteBook 286/12, 1MB, 20MB, Mono/VGA

This type of PC falls into the medium price range. It has extra memory capacity (1MB) and will easily run a word processor and a low-level desktop publishing program such as First Publisher or Publish It!. This notebook computer supports a monochrome video mode that can display images in VGA resolutions. (Additional discussion of PC display modes is covered in Chapter 9, "PC Monitors and Printers.")

A student might elect to go with a portable bubble-jet printer. This type of printer also operates from batteries, is lightweight, and produces excellent printed documents. With a desktop publisher and this printer, a student can publish reports that include both text and graphics. The system described here (notebook computer, bubble-jet printer, and rechargeable batteries) would weigh about 12 pounds.

A PC for a Publisher

A publisher with a design and desktop publishing (DTP) business will want to provide customers with a complete range of DTP services, including the creation of color presentation products such as slides and overhead projection materials. To do this, a publisher would need to use some high-end commercial software packages that require plenty of memory and a fast, powerful PC.

Because a publisher works with large documents, it would make sense to buy a high-resolution monitor that allows two pages of text to display on one screen. A publisher might want to use a high-capacity hard disk to store both programs and data files and have a high-quality color printer. In addition, the graphics services a publisher provides might require a scanner. A *scanner* is a device that can electronically scan text and graphics images into the computer. Once an image is scanned, the publisher can use a PC's graphics programs to manipulate the image into a final form for DTP operations.

A PC system for desktop publishing is a high-priced setup. The description of a publisher's basic PC platform might be as follows:

DTPPC 386/33 (64KB cache), 8MB (exp. 16MB), 200MB, SVGA

This PC has a 386 CPU running at a fast clock speed (33MHz). It has 8MB (expandable to 16MB) of memory and a large hard disk (200MB). It is capable of displaying colors in super VGA (SVGA) mode. SVGA mode lets you work with high-resolution images that contain hundreds of colors. (PC display modes are covered further in Chapter 9, "PC Monitors and Printers.")

What is the reference to "cache" in the preceding PC description? On more powerful PCs, a small amount of additional, very fast memory is provided. This additional memory, or *cache memory*, is designed to store data that the PC uses most often. When the most frequently used data is cached, the PC's operations are sped up considerably. On less powerful PCs without hardware cache features, caching can still be done. There are several PC utility programs available to help a user reserve portions of memory for caching operations.

The PC Adventures of a Computer Game Player

A computer game player is likely to own all types of entertainment software, including simulations, fantasy adventures, and fast-paced arcade games. The game player's PC is equipped with specialized pointing devices, such as a joystick, a trackball, and a games' controller, which make it possible to play games without touching the keyboard. To hear the full effect of the sounds that go along with each game, a game player must install a sound board in his or her PC. That board produces high-quality, stereo audio output that can be listened to with a set of headphones or directed to the speaker systems on a home entertainment system.

A typical game player's PC would be in the low- to medium-price range and can be described as follows:

GAMEPC 386SX/16, 1MB, 80MB, SVGA

This PC includes super VGA color capability. Future games will fully utilize that color mode. This system has a hard disk because most of the good games play better that way and many need a hard disk to store the entire program. Game operations, especially the display of graphics images, are faster with a hard disk drive.

A computer game player eventually might want to acquire a compact disc (CD) drive for this PC when there are enough games available on that type of medium.

A PC for a Salesperson

A salesperson's computer work, like that of a college student, can lend itself to a portable PC. A salesperson traveling to different offices and locations to make sales presentations could use a lightweight, portable PC that is moderately fast.

A salesperson who needs a portable might want to consider buying a notebook PC with the following characteristics:

PCSHOW 386SX/16, 4MB, 80MB, Mono/VGA

Notice that this notebook PC is similar to the game player's desktop PC, except that it has more memory and both monochrome and VGA video display capabilities. When making presentations, the salesperson can use an external color monitor if one is available. Otherwise, he or she can rely on the PC's monochrome display and direct the screen images onto a wall by using a portable projection system that attaches to the computer.

Even though this system is functionally similar to the game player's system, this one will cost slightly more since it is a notebook PC and has more memory. In addition, the buyer of this system would also incur the cost of the projection device used to display the screen images on a wall. This PC system falls into the medium- to high-cost range.

The PCs in a Teacher's Classroom

Teachers have computing needs that differ from those of many PC users. A teacher may need one or more PCs in the classroom and perhaps a PC to carry home. An answer to these dual needs is to have a medium-cost notebook PC to use and carry around and low-cost desktop PCs in the classroom.

The characteristics of a teacher's notebook PC might be the same as those in the college student's example, listed previously:

NoteBook 286/12, 1MB, 20MB, Mono/VGA

A teacher can use the same operating environment on three desktop PCs for the classroom as on a portable PC. Three classroom PCs might have the following characteristics:

ClassPC 286/12, 1MB, 40MB, VGA (one unit)
ClassPC 286/12, 1MB, Mono (two units)

The classroom PCs are low-cost 286 computers. One PC with a hard disk and a color monitor could be used as the main classroom computer. Two monochrome PCs with only floppy disks could be used as word processing stations as well as learning stations for less colorful, educational software. Everyone in the classroom could share a printer connected through a rotary switch. The switch would allow any computer to access the printer, including the teacher's notebook PC.

The choice of classroom hardware is made, in part, by the school's budget, and a decision to go with monochrome rather than color at the other two stations might be the only way to afford the hard disk capability for one system. Eventually, the purchase of an inexpensive network system could link the classroom units together. In that way, all the computers would be able to share the hard disk on the main classroom unit.

A PC for a Writer

A professional writer may write stories, articles, books, and occasional letters to friends and critics. For such tasks it would be beneficial to have a high-end word processor with several support programs such as a spelling checker, a thesaurus, and a grammar and style checker. A writer may want to maintain voluminous files of research data on everything he or she writes about using a sophisticated database program to search and retrieve information. A writer may also have an idea processor, a program that helps generate and organize ideas in order to script stories and plots, or a specialized plot generation program to break through occasional periods of writer's block.

A successful writer might want to print drafts and final copy on a high-quality laser printer or use an electronic scanner to move text information directly from newspaper clippings and magazine articles into electronic files. A writer could also benefit from having a compact disc (CD) drive and several CDs of encyclopedic information and writers' tools. Since a writer often has the freedom to work out of the home, he or she can communicate with editors, an agent, and the rest of the outside world with the use of a telephone, a PC, and a combination modem/fax device.

In order to accomplish these tasks, a writer would require a system with moderate computing power, and could get by with a medium-priced, reasonably fast PC that has a hard disk. A writer's PC system of choice might be as follows:

WritePC 386/16, 1MB (exp. 4MB), 80MB, Mono/VGA

This system shows a VGA capability. Does a writer need color? Probably not, but since writers look at the screen a lot, the best choice would be a high-resolution monochrome system that operates in VGA mode. This feature offers the capability of displaying highly readable text pages on the monitor.

A Fast PC for a Mathematician

Consider what type of computer would be required for a mathematician who builds large-scale computer models as part of work involving theoretical physics. Such work could involve the study of three dimensional graphics images and mathematical objects called fractals. *Fractals* can be used to create complex and beautiful computer graphic images. The generation of fractals and other elaborate graphics images requires a high-cost, state-of-the-art PC with a lot of computer power.

A description of the PC required for these types of calculations and displays is as follows:

PCPOWER 486/50 (256KB cache), 8MB, 200MB, SVGA

This PC has a 486 chip running at a fast clock speed (50MHz). It has a large cache memory area (256KB) and operates with 8MB of regular memory. It has a 200MB hard disk, and supports a super VGA mode color display.

A person doing this type of work would need a laser printer for high-quality output. In addition, a high-quality color printer would be useful for printing some of the more interesting images in color. (Additional discussions of printers and printer quality issues are covered in Chapter 9, "PC Monitors and Printers.")

Few home and business users are likely to need a PC as powerful as this. Of course, in a few years, a PC like this will be considered either an antique or the equivalent of today's low-end system as newer and more powerful chips and technologies are developed.

Everybody's Home PC

The home PC system is often used for a variety of computing tasks. It can be used as a general-purpose productivity device to help people keep records, do calculations, and write letters and reports. At other times, the family uses it as an entertainment device. They play games and solve puzzles and use it to draw colorful graphics images.

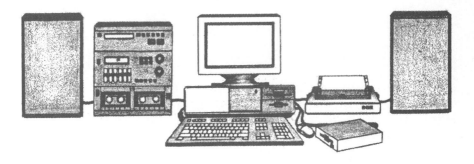

On other occasions, individuals use the PC to help them learn. They study languages, brush up on their math skills, and browse historical information. Occasionally, the PC and an attached modem get used for telecommunications. The family PC is linked with other PCs, electronic messages are sent and received, and one or more commercial information services, such as PC Link, Prodigy, GEnie, or CompuServe, is accessed.

As you can tell, the home PC needs to be flexible and expandable. Since the family members use the system for entertainment, they definitely want good color and stereo sound. Because they use the system for productivity, learning, communications, and entertainment, they no doubt have many software programs. This means that they can make good use of a hard disk.

The family's home PC system would be something like the following:

HomePC 386SX/16, 1MB (exp. 4MB), 40MB, SVGA

The key elements in the choice of a PC home system are

- Having the ability to meet the family's total range of computing tasks

- Providing enough power, storage capacity, and color to support the types of computing being done

- Being expandable to accommodate future computing needs

This PC system for the home would most likely have a 24-pin or bubble-jet printer, a mouse, a sound board, and enough expansion slots to add future devices such as a compact disc (CD) drive or music board.

Summary of Selecting PC Hardware Systems

As you can see from this chapter, every computing situation comes with its own set of requirements. The PC hardware and software system chosen to meet specific needs can be tailored to closely match what is required.

Your particular computing needs probably fall somewhere in between two or more of the scenarios that have been presented. After reading through all of the examples, pick two or more that address some of the tasks you want to accomplish with a PC.

It is important to realize that 8086- and 8088-based computers will not run many of the software packages available today, such as Windows and OS/2 applications. In addition, it is probable that some software in the future will not support the 80286 computers. If your interest is expandability into the future, you should strongly consider buying at least an 80386 computer. The 80386 computers will likely serve you well for the next several years, and prices for the 80386SX computers are not much different from 80286 computers.

As you consider the examples given in this chapter, study what you would have to change to get the exact system you need by asking yourself the following questions. Do you require more computing power? Can you get that by keeping the same CPU and increasing the clock speed? Or should you simply go for a more powerful processing chip? How much data will you be storing? How big a hard disk drive will you need? Do you need color? Sound? What type of printer is going to work for you—a 24-pin dot-matrix, bubble-jet, or laser printer? Do you need a modem? A mouse?

Using the scenarios as a guide, write down what you think will be true for you. Use this information as a starting point when you begin to talk with computer store salespeople or start to browse the advertisements for mail-order equipment.

Check with friends and coworkers who already have computers and see what you can learn. Go to a local user group meeting and see if the conclusions you are coming to make sense to people there. Finally, of course, you will have to make your own decisions. But the process outlined in this chapter will give you confidence that you have approached the issues thoughtfully. You have learned to ask intelligent questions and can now understand the answers, including many of the more technical responses.

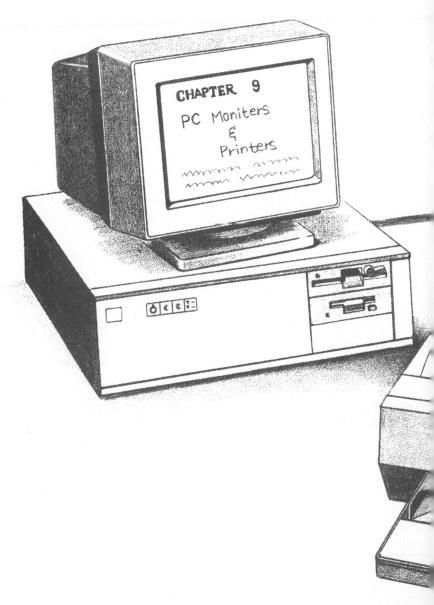

CHAPTER 9

PC Moniters
&
Printers

PC Monitors
and Printers

CHAPTER 9
PC Monitors
&
Printers

This chapter gives you additional information about selecting PC monitors and printers. Although there are many different companies producing these devices, your choices are simplified here. To be competitive, monitor and printer manufacturers must adhere to technological industry standards regarding these products. Because of the standards, you need to concentrate only on a limited set of criteria when making monitor and printer selection decisions.

PC Monitors

The PC monitor, working with a PC display adapter, translates the video signals coming from the computer into images on the screen. The *display adapter* is a controller that re-sides inside the chassis of the PC. It helps route the PC's video signals to the monitor. The type of display adapter and monitor being used deter-mines the sharpness, resolu-tion, and color of the displayed images.

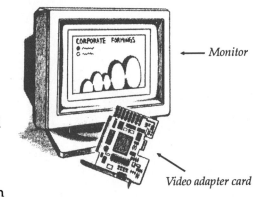

←——— *Monitor*

Video adapter card

Sharpness is how clear a dis-played image is when viewed on the screen. Fuzzy images can result when you use poor-quality monitors or low-resolution display adapters.

Resolution involves the number of dots, or *pixels*, that can be displayed on the screen. The number of pixels is usually discussed in terms of the amount of dots that fit across and down the screen. For example, a typical VGA monitor has a resolution of 640 pixels across by 480 pixels down the screen (640x480 = 307,200 pixels).

Low resolution

Higher resolution

PC Display Modes

The code letters for the various display adapters are based on historical and current PC video standards. MDA stands for monochrome display adapter, CGA for color graphics adapter, and EGA for enhanced graphics adapter. VGA, a popular current standard, is the abbreviation for video graphics adapter. The most recent video display standard is Super VGA, or super video graphics adapter.

MDA-, CGA-, and EGA-style monitors and display adapters are now industry antiques. Newer PCs and current software products are being designed to take advantage of the higher resolution and sharper images produced with VGA and Super VGA technologies.

Even users who do not need color are discovering that VGA features are easier on the eyes. When displayed in VGA, video color signals on a monochrome PC monitor are translated into shades of gray. The resultant images are sharp, clear, and high quality, based on VGA's better resolution.

Software/Hardware Compatibility

What happens when you try to operate older software, written to run in MDA, CGA, or EGA display mode, on a system with VGA or Super VGA capabilities? In general, PCs with VGA and Super VGA

capabilities will still
run software designed to run under older standards. VGA and Super VGA are said to be *backward compatible* with previous video display modes.

Standard VGA resolution is 640x480 pixels. However, you can find VGA monitors and adapters with a wide range of horizontal and vertical pixel arrangements. If you encounter a monitor with a nonstandard resolution, make sure your PC's display adapter works with the monitor. A low price for the monitor is of no value if images cannot be displayed or if the images are fuzzy and difficult to see.

The Super VGA standard includes two resolutions: 800x600 pixels and 1024x768 pixels. You can find Super VGA equipment that conforms to either one or both of these standards. If you plan to use a high-end GUI, such as Windows, you are strongly encouraged to have at least a Super VGA system with 800x600 pixel resolution.

If you use a variety of software packages written to run in a range of display modes, you may want to investigate the advantages of having a multiscanning display. *Multiscanning monitors,* which automatically adjust the display to the resolutions of the incoming video signals, are available. In fact, there are quite expensive multiscanning monitors that work with resolutions beyond the upper limits of Super VGA capabilities. VGA and Super VGA monitors and adapters that do not multiscan are less expensive than multiscanning units. However, multiscanning units give you flexibility into the future as new software products take advantage of the improved resolution of newer PCs.

Monitor Size

Monitor sizes, like television set sizes, are stated in terms of inches. The quoted sizes refer to the diagonal distances across the faces of the display tubes.

PC monitors come in a range of sizes from 9 inches to large-screen units of over 30 inches. The bulk of the more common, and more affordable, monitors are in the 14- to 16-inch range.

Will a larger sized monitor automatically give you better images? Not necessarily. A larger monitor will give you a larger, but not always sharper, image. Image sharpness, although related to monitor size, is more a function of the

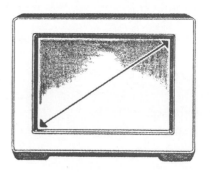

Measurement of monitor size

monitor's resolution (number of pixels) and how closely spaced the dots of color are on the screen. The spacing of color dots is referred to as a monitor's *dot pitch* capability.

A monitor's dot pitch, expressed in terms of millimeters per dot, establishes the ultimate sharpness of a display device. For example, there are inexpensive monitors that technically match VGA resolution standards (640x480 pixels) but have coarse dot-pitch characteristics (.50mm or more per dot). A 14-inch VGA monitor needs a minimum dot pitch of about .40mm to produce sharp images. To satisfy this type of requirement across all monitors, most high-quality displays are designed to conform to an accepted dot pitch standard of .31mm or less.

Dot pitch at different resolutions

If you plan to use Super VGA resolutions, especially the high-resolution mode (1024x768 pixels), you may need to get a slightly bigger monitor. Look into 14- to 16-inch monitors with dot-pitch characteristics of .28mm or less.

You can find monitors larger than 16 inches with good dot-pitch characteristics, but be prepared for a significant price jump over 12- to 16-inch units. A really large monitor (over 20 inches) can cost more than the rest of your PC system.

PC Printers

The device you connect to your PC that lets you print on paper the images and information you see on your monitor is called a *printer*. The three most common types of printers are dot-matrix, ink-jet, and laser printers.

Dot-matrix Printers

Dot-matrix printers provide a low-cost way to produce documents with letter-quality (LQ) or near-letter-quality (NLQ) characteristics. Each character printed by these printers is formed by an arrangement of dots within a rectangular array, or *matrix*. The total number of dots used in the matrix determines the quality of the printed image.

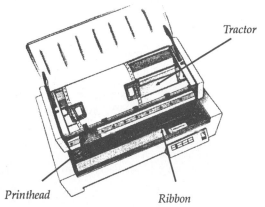

Tractor

Printhead

Ribbon

Dot-matrix printer

Dot-matrix printers produce letters or images by striking the paper with small pins within the printhead. It is for this reason that these devices are referred to as *impact printers.* Unless they are enclosed in noise-reducing enclosures, impact printers usually make more noise than nonimpact ink-jet and laser printers.

The printheads in most dot-matrix printers use either 9 or 24 pins. The 24-pin printers produce the highest quality images and letters. The larger number of smaller pins in a 24-pin printhead creates smoother looking printed patterns. Some 9-pin printers achieve nearly the same results by making multiple print passes combined with a slight shifting of the printhead position. However, multiple passes slow down the printing process. A 24-pin printer can do the job faster. Also, multiple passes of a slower, 9-pin printer mean that you hear more printer noise for a longer period of time.

9-pin

24-pin

Most of today's dot-matrix printers provide built-in capabilities to reproduce **boldface,** <u>underlined</u>, and *italicized* letters. In some cases, you may find printers that support subscripts (H_2O), superscripts (x^2), and overstrike features (café). A few dot-matrix printers even give you the ability to select different fonts in a variety of sizes, like this:

Hi   Hi   *Hi*

If you think you will need these types of printer features, carefully evaluate the printers you are considering before making a final selection.

To generate the highest quality graphics images on a dot-matrix printer, you will probably want to use a 24-pin device. The smaller pin size of a 24-pin printer, combined with the printer's ability to shift and adjust the positioning of each dot, results in detailed images. The dots in such images, which number hundreds of dots per inch, become smoothly overlapped and solid looking.

However, if you plan to print many graphics images, you will want to examine the quieter, and faster, ink-jet and laser printers.

Ink-jet Printers

Ink-jet printers use electrically charged streams of ink particles to create dot-matrix printed images. Ink-jet printers are quieter than conventional dot-matrix devices since the ink-jet printer does not use a printhead that strikes the paper.

Ink-jet printer image

The print quality of an ink-jet printer is almost as good as that found with laser printers. Ink-jet printers are much faster than dot-matrix printers that have to rely on multiple passes to achieve better levels of print quality. In many cases, ink-jet printers are even faster than laser printers when printing graphics images. However, laser printers are faster when it comes to printing text.

Lightweight, portable, battery-powered ink-jet printers have recently become available. These compact, notebook-sized units provide high-quality printer capabilities at surprisingly low costs. If you have limited desk space or need to carry your printer to a variety of locations, an ink-jet printer may be the answer.

Portable ink-jet printer

Laser Printers

Laser printers produce the highest quality, highest resolution printed materials. Laser printers rely on technologies associated with copy machines. With a high-resolution monitor and a laser printer, you can turn your PC into a local publishing operation.

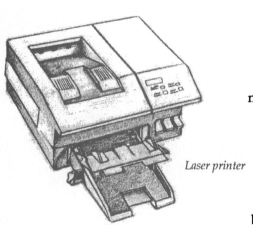

Laser printer

Of the three types of printers, laser units are the most expensive. Because they print an entire page at once, laser printers are generally faster than ink-jet or dot-matrix devices.

In the world of laser printers, you will find two basic types of units: PCL and PostScript laser printers. *PCL* and *PostScript* are the names of the two most common printer control languages. A *printer control language* controls the transfer of information from the computer to the printed page.

PostScript laser printers are more flexible than PCL-driven units, but usually you have to pay more for PostScript capabilities. PostScript describes to the printer how an entire page is to be printed. One result is that PostScript-driven printers can produce better quality graphics than PCL devices. Another consideration is that most typesetting operations can deal only with PostScript files. Commercial typesetting houses have not established a convenient method of processing PCL files into final typeset images.

PostScript and PCL printers are nearly the same in terms of hardware components. The basic difference comes down to the language (software) being used to control the printer. It is possible to upgrade many PCL devices to PostScript capabilities. To do so, you usually have to put extra memory and a PostScript board into the printer and add PostScript printer control software to your system.

For many home and small business users, a PCL laser printer will meet your needs. If your needs expand, you can upgrade to PostScript when the situation arises. If you are using your PC for professional publication work, you will want to start out with a PostScript-equipped printer. Cost considerations will ultimately dictate the path you choose.

More About Printers

A basic PC printer may require additional pieces of hardware to work well in your environment. For example, most printers move paper past the printhead by using either a trac-tor or friction feed

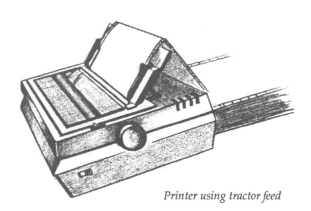

Printer using tractor feed

mechanism. A *tractor feed* is used for continuous forms. The tractor is a device with a set of sprockets that fit into holes along the edges of the paper. A *friction feed*, which operates like the roller on typewriters, is used for single pages.

Most dot-matrix and ink-jet printers provide both types of feeder options. However, on some dot-matrix and ink-jet printers, a tractor feed is optional and has to be purchased separately. Laser printers rely mostly on friction feed to move paper through the units.

If you plan to print a lot on single sheets, you may need to acquire a sheet feeder. *Sheet feeders* are designed to feed stacks of single pages (and sometimes envelopes) into the printer's friction-feed mechanism. Most laser printers come with one cartridge unit that lets you feed a stack of standard pages into the unit. To use other paper sizes and envelopes, you may have to purchase separate cartridges or feed units.

If you need to print in color, you have several options. Some dot-matrix printers give you limited color capabilities based on the use of special printer ribbons. Two- and three-color ribbons combined with the printer's overstrike features can generate impressive, but limited, colored images.

You can produce limited color images with laser printers by changing the ink cartridges. To get multiple colors, you have to run the pages through the printer several times. More elaborate, and more expensive, color printers are available, which use a wax-based ink. The ink is melted off the ribbon and transferred onto the page by means of a variation of the ink-jet technology. The resultant color images are impressive in terms of both quality and color reproduction. An additional benefit of these printers is that they are extremely quiet.

Other PC Peripherals

In this chapter, you learn about additional hardware devices that you can add to your PC system. Other hardware units, or *peripheral devices*, can extend and enhance the capabilities of your PC. The following devices are discussed:

- Keyboards

- Pointing devices

- External data storage devices

- Communications devices

- Scanners

Keyboards

Not all keyboards are created equal. Some keyboards are smaller and have fewer keys than others. Some keyboards have additional keys designed to help you perform specific tasks on the computer. The keyboard that comes as standard equipment with a desktop PC may be completely satisfactory, but you still have the option of choosing different model keyboards if you do not like the standard unit or have special computing needs. Of course, you may have to pay extra for a nonstandard model.

IBM enhanced keyboard

Most desktop PCs come with a keyboard that looks similar to an IBM enhanced keyboard, which has 101 keys, including a row of function keys across the top of the unit, a set of cursor control keys, a set of editing keys, and a full function numeric keypad. For most people, this style of keyboard works well and does not need to be replaced.

Specialized keyboards can be found that have the following features:

- Additional keys that produce special characters
- Additional function keys
- Additional cursor movement keys
- Additional editing and control keys
- Built-in calculators and pointing devices
- Keys that can be customized to your computing needs

When you look for an alternate keyboard, try to verify that the model you like works with your PC. Make sure you have a money-back guarantee in case you find that a chosen keyboard fails to function with your computer.

Pointing Devices

PC pointing devices let you direct the actions of the computer without touching the keyboard. There are several different types of pointing devices; each type has evolved to satisfy specific computing needs.

The Mouse

A *mouse* is a palm-sized device with a roller or ball on its bottom surface and one to three buttons on its top. You roll the mouse around on a flat surface—either on a smooth desk-top area or on a mouse pad. A *mouse pad* is a cushioned, textured patch of material on which you roll the mouse. The textured surface of the pad lets you precisely control a mouse's movements.

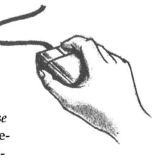

Mouse

Movements of a mouse are translated into movements of a screen pointer on the PC monitor. When you press a button on the mouse, that action translates into an action on the screen, determined by the program being used and the position of the screen pointer.

The creation of graphics software helped popularize the use of a mouse in computing. Although it is possible to draw images by using the keyboard, it simply is not efficient. More recently, the introduction of sophisticated GUIs and commercial software have almost made a mouse a necessity. Many PC manufacturers now include a mouse as standard equipment.

From a hardware standpoint, there are two types of mice: bus and serial. Using a *bus mouse* requires putting a board in one of the expansion slots in your PC. With a *serial mouse,* you connect the mouse through a serial port on the back of the PC. There is no appreciable operational difference between the two types of units. A bus mouse frees a serial port for other devices but uses up one expansion slot.

There are two types of mouse technologies: mechanical and optical. *Mechanical mice* use a roller ball and sensors inside the mouse bodies to track movements. *Optical mice* use special mouse pads with reflecting surfaces to track movements and to sense a mouse's location.

As mice have become standard equipment on newer PCs, mouse prices have dropped. You can add a high-quality mouse to your PC for less than $100.

Trackballs

A *trackball* is a pointing device that uses a ball mounted on top of a unit that stays in one place. You rest your hand on the base of the trackball and use your fingers or hand to move the ball. When the ball moves, the pointer on the screen follows the movements of the ball.

Standard trackball

Like a mouse, a trackball has one or more buttons on top of the device. When a screen pointer is positioned with the ball and a button is clicked, or pressed, the program performs whatever action is indicated based on the location of the pointer.

You can use trackball units to perform fast—and very precise—screen pointer movements. For this reason, trackballs are used to control entertainment software and applications that involve precision movements of objects on the screen.

Trackballs stay in a fixed position and take up much less desk space than a mouse. Trackballs can also be moved off the desk top. You can hold them in your hand, place them on the arm of your chair, or place them beside you within easy reach.

In general, a mouse and a trackball perform nearly the same functions in terms of directing activities on a PC screen. You will find it a bit easier to draw images using a mouse than using a trackball. However, most professional computer artists prefer to use a pen-based pointing device rather than a mouse or a trackball (see the next section).

A type of miniature trackball now exists that attaches to the edge of the keyboard on notebook computers. You can operate this pointing device with one hand without removing your other hand from the keyboard.

Trackball for notebook PC

Pens and Tablets

Most computer artists and a number of regular computer users prefer to use pointing devices that have the look and feel of a pencil or pen. Many artists prefer to draw images on the screen in the same way they learned to draw on paper. They find a mouse or trackball awkward to use.

Pen-based systems include light-sensitive pens that are used directly on the surface of the monitor.

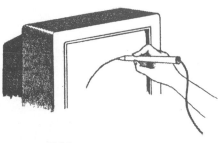

Light pen

A *light pen*, as this type of pointing device is called, lets a user interact with objects on the monitor as if he or she were working on a canvas. Images can be drawn, edited, moved, and erased with easy movements of the pen. With a light pen, the user appears to be using the screen just like a piece of paper.

There are also pen, or stylus, systems that rely on a sensitized tablet. The tablet sits on the desk, next to the PC. The user moves a pen, stylus, or finger across the tablet's surface. The tablet detects the position and movement of the pen. The pen's motions are sent to the computer, where they get translated into movements of objects on the screen. Drawing with a sensitized tablet is exactly like drawing on a piece of paper. In fact, images placed on the tablet and traced can be transmitted to the screen. Even non-artists are able to generate amazing graphics images using a pen and tablet system.

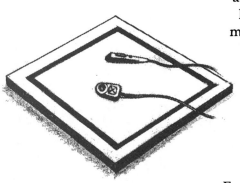

Pen and tablet system

The latest versions of pen and tablet systems are quite sophisticated. Some units detect the position of the pen as long as it is above the tablet; the two items do not have to be in contact. This allows a user to direct the screen pointer quickly around the screen and initiate actions with a precision, accuracy, and efficiency that surpass other pointing-device capabilities. These advantages do not come without costs. Pen and tablet systems are among the most expensive types of PC pointing devices.

External Data Storage Devices

In addition to a PC's built-in floppy and hard drives, you can attach external data storage devices to your computer. You can add external floppy disks, hard disks, bulk storage drives with removable cartridges, CD drives, and tape backup devices.

External Floppy and Hard Drives

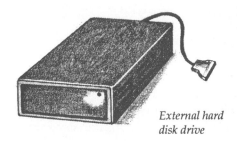

External hard disk drive

As you use your PC, you may discover you need more data storage capacity. To increase your PC's storage volume, you can acquire a second hard drive. For a PC already filled with drives and boards, a second hard drive can be attached by cable and put outside the chassis.

You may also want to add an external floppy drive to your system. For example, you may have an internal 5 1/4 -inch floppy drive and find that you also need to use 3 1/2-inch disks. Attaching an external 3 1/2-inch drive to your system solves the problem.

External hard and floppy drives cost slightly more than internal units because of their housings and cables. Although you may never need to do so, you can attach dozens of external disk drives to any PC that has sufficient expansion slots. The slots are needed for the boards used to control the external drives.

Removable Bulk Storage Units

Early PC users quickly realized that it would be handy to have a data storage device with features of both floppy and hard disks. They wanted a unit with the capacity of a hard drive where the disk component could be easily removed or exchanged. One answer to that need is the *cartridge disk drive*. This device features a removable cartridge that has the data storage capacity of a small hard disk.

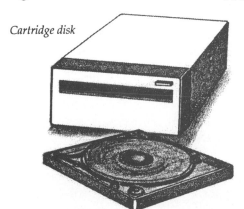

Cartridge disk

CD Drives

Audio compact discs (CDs) have virtually displaced records in music stores. A technical relative of these discs, called a *CD-ROM*, has found its way into the computer arena. A CD-ROM accommodates the storage of large amounts of text information and limited graphics. The immense, optically encoded storage capacities of this medium seem a natural match with the information-processing powers of a PC.

CD   =   450 books   =   over 300,000 pages   =   over 50 disks

Although this is a relatively new technology, there are already hundreds of CD-ROM titles available. You can purchase reference materials, databases, games, software programs, and learning products in the CD-ROM format. You can find complete PC systems that come bundled with a CD-ROM drive and several CD-ROM titles. When you purchase a CD-ROM drive by itself, you often have the option of obtaining a collection of CD-ROM titles at a significant discount.

The most recent innovation in CD technologies involves an alternative CD format called CD-I (for CD-Interactive). CD-I can store both text, graphics, and motion video. The CD-I format lets users fully interact with the stored images and information, limited only by the speed of the PC and the access time of the CD-I drives. At present, there are dozens of CD-I titles that can be played on a PC outfitted with a CD-I drive.

Tape Backup Systems

If you have one or more large-volume hard disks, backing up your information onto dozens of floppy disks can be a chore. One solution is to use a tape backup unit.

A tape backup system lets you quickly save and restore many megabytes of information in minutes instead of hours. If you need to routinely save the information on your hard disks, investigate this reliable and inexpensive data storage alternative.

Tape backup system

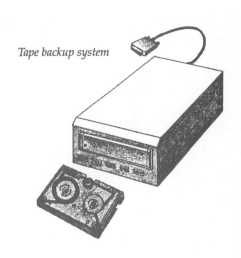

If you want to move data between two PCs with a tape system, both computers will need the same tape unit. There is no guarantee that different tape storage systems can read each other's tapes.

PC Communications Devices

You can use your PC to send information to another computer or electronic device. Similarly, your PC can receive electronic information from a variety of sources.

One way to turn your PC into a communications station is to use a peripheral device called a *modem*. A modem lets you communicate with other modem-equipped computers either

Modem

directly or by using telephone lines. A modem, working in conjunction with a telecommunications program, converts information from your PC to signals that can travel over the telephone. The same piece of equipment also decodes incoming telephone signals, turning those signals back into electronic computer data.

The speed at which a modem transmits and receives data is referred to as its *bit rate*. A bit rate of 10 corresponds to a transmission rate of 1 character per second, a bit rate of 300 to 30 characters per second. Bit rate is also referred to in terms of the numbers of bits per second (bps) being transmitted. Thus, a bit rate of 300 is also referred to as 300 bps.

In general, the faster the modem, the more its initial cost. A faster modem, however, saves you time and, if you are paying telephone line charges, might save you money.

The following list shows how long it takes to transmit or receive one typewritten page of information at various bit rates. One page is assumed to be 4800 characters (60 lines with 80 characters per line, including spaces).

Bit Rate	Transfer Time
300	160 seconds
1200	40 seconds
2400	20 seconds
4800	10 seconds
9600	5 seconds

PC equipment that combines the functions of a modem and a fax machine is also available. With this type of hardware, you can send and receive computer files as well as facsimiles. The fax images are transmitted directly to and from your computer's disk without the need for a separate fax unit. Any fax you receive this way can be viewed on the monitor and printed on your printer. However, you cannot edit or use the text on an electronic fax image unless you have an optical character recognition (OCR) program. Also, it is not easy for you to sign an electronic fax before shipping it from your PC.

More sophisticated modem/fax units let you handle all your communication needs with your PC. They include features to record, play back, store, and edit voice messages as well as regular electronic computer transmissions.

Scanners

A *scanner* is a PC peripheral that can be used to scan and save both printed and hand-drawn information. Scanners come in two types of physical units: hand-held and flatbed, or full-page.

You operate a hand-held scanner by moving the small (approximately palm-sized) unit down the page of material to be scanned. Hand-held scanners work best on small images and document areas. Using this type of scanner requires a steady hand.

Hand-held scanner

A flatbed or full-page scanner operates like a copy machine. You place the page to be scanned on the top, flat surface of the scanner. The scanner then scans the information on the page into the computer. Flatbed scanners produce the best quality of scanned images.

Scanners that handle a variety of scanning tasks also can be found. Scanners have been designed to scan color images, graphics, text, and combinations of these three items. Text scanners are often mated with OCR software that converts the scanned images into text files for use in a word processor.

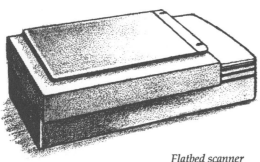

Flatbed scanner

Scanners, like printers and monitors, work in resolutions defined in terms of the number of dots per inch that the scanner can produce. The higher the resolution (the more dots per inch), the more costly the scanner. Flatbed scanners cost more than hand-held units. Also, color scanners are more expensive than devices that produce black-and-white images.

In addition, accurate, fast, and flexible OCR software may cost as much as or more than the scanner itself. Before investing in a scanner and supporting software packages, locate people who already use such equipment and products. Ask them to show you what their systems can do and where their setups fail to work for them. DTP service bureaus can be good sources of information about scanners and related software.

Recently, several low-cost scanners with built-in OCR capabilities have appeared on the market. One hand-held unit, which is called The Typist, has garnered rave reviews and points to the way of the future in scanning technologies.

A Final Word About PC Peripherals

As you begin to explore adding peripherals to your PC system, take time to research your alternatives. Make sure the features you need in a peripheral exist in the units you are considering. Also, do a lot of comparison shopping. Changes in technology quickly transform yesterday's expensive items into tomorrow's bargains. This cautionary note applies in particular to the acquisition of printers, monitors, large-volume hard disk drives, and scanning equipment and related software.

Acquiring and Maintaining Your System

In this chapter, you explore several important items and issues that can affect you as you begin to acquire and assemble your PC system. The information is organized into sections that deal with various aspects of acquiring and maintaining a PC.

Acquiring Software

Suppose you have found a PC software program you wish to acquire. You have seen demonstrations of the program in operation. You have talked with friends who own the package and gathered their impressions and opinions. The program is on sale at your local computer store. The sales price closely matches what you would pay by ordering from a mail-order house. You are standing in the store with the package in your hands.

Do you need to know anything else before you make the purchase? The answer is yes. You need to determine if the program will run on *your* PC and if you are buying the most recent version of the product.

Will the Program Run on Your PC?

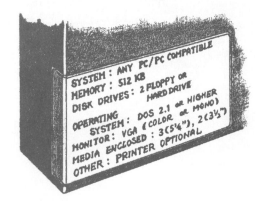

Examine the outside of the package you plan to buy. Most commercial software programs clearly exhibit a list of minimum require- ments to use the product. You should find the follow- ing information:

PC compatibility guide	A list of PCs on which the program is guar- anteed to run
Memory requirements	The minimum amount of memory needed for the program to operate

Disk drives	The minimum number of drive(s) needed and the type of drive required (floppy or hard disk)
Operating environment	The operating system (DOS, GUI, and so forth) used to run the program
Other hardware requirements	A list of printers, video modes (VGA, SVGA, and so forth), sound boards, pointing devices, and other hardware units that the product requires or supports
Media	An indication of which size disks are in the package (3 1/2-inch, 5 1/4-inch)

Look carefully through the program's list of requirements and compatibilities. If you have a PC with 1MB of memory, you may want to reconsider buying a program that requires 2MB of memory. To run such a program, you would have to purchase additional memory for your PC.

If you have no hard disk and the program runs only on PCs with hard disks, you may want to rethink your choice of software. Do you need the program enough to warrant the acquisition of a hard disk on which to run it?

If you have questions, ask the store personnel to help you determine if the program is going to work for you. Also ask about the store's return policy should you discover that you cannot use the package.

Which Version Are You Getting?

As newer versions of a product are released, older versions are sometimes discounted and put on sale. In general, you'll want the latest version of a product unless the newer product requires that you expand your PC's hardware.

A product's version number may appear on the outside of its package. Occasionally, you have to open the package and run the software to locate the version number. If you are in a software store, ask the salesperson to help you find the product's version number. Also ask about upcoming product revisions. Most software companies let existing product users

upgrade to newer versions for a fee that is much less than purchasing the latest product. Version numbers usually appear in one of the following formats: v3.5, V3.5, Ver. 3.5, or Version 3.5. In some instances, products have a release number instead of a version number. In that situation, the release number formats would be as follows: r3.5, R3.5, Rel. 3.5, or Release 3.5.

Here is how you interpret a version or release number:

- The digit *before* the decimal point indicates which *major* product revision you have.

- The digit *after* the decimal point indicates the number of *minor* revisions that have been made to the current major revision.

For example, Ver. 3.5 of a program means that this is the third major version of the product and that there have been five minor revisions to this third version. Occasionally, you will see a third digit in the version number (v3.51). This means that there have been two very minor corrections made to the last (fifth) minor revision.

If two completely different software packages have the same version number, you cannot infer anything from that coincidence except that both products have had the same number of revisions. If a product version number starts with zero (0.*xx*), it usually indicates a product that is being tested and has not been released commercially.

Licenses and Registration

Each commercial software package contains some form of *licensing agreement*. This agreement spells out your rights as a purchaser and user of the software. The agreement also establishes the limits of liabilities and services provided by the product manufacturer.

Read the agreement carefully, and if required, send in any registration materials included in the package once you know the software runs on your PC. Often, any support or services offered by the manufacturer, or any warranty periods and upgrade offers, are tied to the product being properly registered.

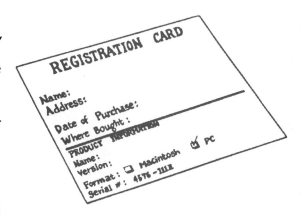

Software Piracy Issues

Each software licensing agreement spells out that manufacturer's position about you making copies of their programs. In general, you are allowed to make backup copies of the original disks, *for your use only.*

Except for shareware products, you are not allowed to copy and distribute a program you buy to your friends, coworkers, or classmates. Copying, distributing, and using such software is illegal. Individuals and entire companies have been cited for piracy activities related to making and using unauthorized copies of software products.

Acquiring Hardware

Ideally, once you have identified the software you plan to use on your PC, you can proceed with the acquisition of the hardware units. If you already have a PC, you will have to tailor your choices of software to match the hardware you currently own or use.

If you are a person who plans to acquire hardware, how should you proceed? You have talked with friends, coworkers, and salespeople. You have read reports and comparisons. You are ready to get a PC. Where do you begin to shop for a system that will meet your needs?

Based on the type of system you want and what you plan to spend, you have several options. A way to characterize the available options is to discuss how much risk is involved. For example, you may want to go with a brand name PC (relatively low risk) rather than one of the many, lesser-known PC compatibles (possible medium risk). You may want to use a vendor who includes training, support, and repairs (low to medium risk) rather than get your PC from an operation that sells only the hardware (medium to high risk). Perhaps you prefer to order your PC from a reputable mail-order house (medium risk) and ignore trying to find a used system (medium to high risk).

High risk in these situations can be translated into a couple of simple measures. One measure might be your frustration level in having equipment not working and not meeting your needs. Another measure might be the loss of your time or money in working around problems that arise.

Warranty Issues

Computer hardware, like other types of electronic equipment, comes with some form of warranty. Units generally carry a manufacturer's warranty. This type of guarantee assures the buyer that the product will operate properly for a specified amount of time after purchase. If the product fails during the warranty period, the manufacturer agrees to repair or replace the unit. Often the buyer is responsible for getting the nonworking unit back to the manufacturer or dealer for repairs or replacements. The period of warranty normally begins when you complete and send back the warranty cards that come with your hardware unit.

In addition to the manufacturer's guarantees, some dealers offer other assurances regarding services and repairs. Occasionally, these additional guarantees are included in the price of the units. More often, you have the option of purchasing a dealer's service agreement for the equipment. The scope of warranty and service agreements varies widely. Before acquiring a piece of hardware, make sure you understand the extent of any warranty or service agreements that accompany your purchase.

Maintaining Software and Hardware

PC hardware devices are sturdy and reliable. With only a minimum of attention, your PC will operate properly for years. PC software, which comes on floppy disks, is more vulnerable to damage than hardware. However, with only a little thought and care, you can keep your software programs safe and operational.

Maintaining Software

The best way to protect your software investment is to make *backup copies* of every program and important data file that you own and create. If allowed by your software licensing agreements, make copies of all master disks that come with each software package. Once you have made copies of everything, put the master disks away in a safe place. Use the copies on your PC. In this way, if a program disk becomes damaged, you can retrieve an operational copy of the program from the master disk.

Store your valuable master disks in a cool, dry, dust-free location. Do not put these disks near any source of magnetic fields (magnets, telephones, or electrical equipment). Do not place heavy or sharp objects on top of your disks or mark on your disks with a pen or sharp instrument.

Another software maintenance issue involves program updates and new product releases. Program updates often contain fixes for problems and, usually, new program features. A new product release is usually a major product revision.

If you receive an update or major product revision, spend some time verifying that this latest version works with the data files created by your older program. Before trying this experiment, back up your data files. When you determine that the new program operates properly, you can replace the old program with the new one. However, as a form of insurance, keep a copy of the old program and data files in a safe place.

Maintaining Hardware

Most hardware systems require little attention or service. As with software, hardware needs to be in a cool, dry, dust-free environment.

Some PC peripherals with mechanical parts, such as printers, may need periodic cleaning and maintenance. Occasionally, a disk drive may get out of alignment and have to be adjusted by a knowledgeable repair person. If you begin to have difficulty with your hard disk drive, take it immediately to someone who knows how to deal with this technology. If possible, back up the information on your hard disk to floppies or tape before you send the unit in for repair.

Perhaps the most frequent causes of PC hardware damage are fluctuations in electrical power and static discharges. You can protect your PC from most electrical power fluctuations by using surge suppressors. These devices isolate the PC from the electrical lines and shut off the power to the PC if the electrical signals get too erratic.

PC damage from static discharges can be minimized. There are antistatic mats to go under your PC and on the floor around your work area. You can also find sprays that help reduce the frequency of static buildup around your equipment.

At some point, you may have to open the chassis on your PC to install a new board or upgrade the components. Make certain everything electrical is unplugged before attempting such installations. Before touching any chips or components, touch the power supply with your bare hands to discharge any static buildup.

Acquiring Supplies

On a PC, the primary supplies are floppy disks, paper, and either ribbons, toner, or toner cartridges for your printer. All of these items can be purchased from a variety of sources: local computer stores, bulk-purchase outlets, mail-order houses, and directly from the manufacturers.

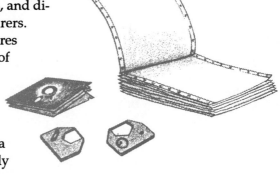

Your local computer stores generally offer a selection of standard supplies. If you have an unusual printer that requires a special ribbon or cartridge, you may have to order it from a mail-order house or directly from the printer manufacturer.

If you use a lot of supplies, you can often save money by buying in larger quantities. The trick with quantity purchases is to make sure that you acquire quality products and that you have room to store the items.

In Appendix D of this book, you will find a list of reputable mail-order houses that offer quality supplies at discount prices. Once you determine your preferred brands, you can order those supplies directly by mail.

In Closing

This book, *Simply PCs*, has taken you on a grand tour of the world of PC computers. You have been introduced to PC software programs and terminology, and to the components of a PC hardware system.

The goal of this book has been to provide you with enough information about PCs so you can continue on your own, confidently. To help you with your future investigations, you will find several appendixes at the end of this book. These appendixes contain lists of resources that will aid you in your subsequent explorations.

PC Magazines
and Books

Two good sources of information about PCs are magazines and books. Magazines help you keep abreast of what is happening in the fast-moving PC industry. They provide up-to-date pricing information, product comparisons and reviews, and articles that help you learn how to better use your PC.

Books provide you with in-depth information about PC software products and hardware systems. PC books cover the gamut from hand-holding texts for beginners to highly technical volumes for sophisticated PC users.

Magazines

There are lots of PC computer magazines. Here is a short list of the authors' favorites. These magazines were very helpful resources while we wrote this book. If you are a beginning PC user, the authors recommend that you look first at those magazines in the following list that are italicized.

Many magazines list a standard subscription rate in the front of their publications. However, look through each one for a "blow-in" card that offers the magazine at a discount. Rates have been included here to provide you with an idea of the relative costs of the named publications. The rates correspond to prices in effect at the time of the printing of this book.

COMPUTE!   General-purpose PC magazine—"Your Complete Home Computer Resource." Departments: Test Lab, Tech Support, Home Office, Discovery, Entertainment, Reviews. Published by COMPUTE Publications International, Ltd., 1965 Broadway, New York, NY 10023-5965. 212-496-6100. Editorial offices: 324 West Endover Avenue, Suite 200, Greensboro, NC 27408. 919-275-9809. Subscriptions: COMPUTE Magazine, P.O. Box 3244, Harlan, IA 51593-2424. 800-727-6937. $19.94/year (12 issues)—blow-in card says $12.97.

Computer Currents   Large-format magazine for somewhat experienced users. Regional editions published 25 times a year in Northern California, Southern California, Georgia, Massachusetts, and Texas. Available free at many local computer stores. Ask about it at your computer stores and magazine stores. Good source of information on computer user groups and bulletin board systems (BBS). Published by Computer Currents Publishing, Inc., 5720 Hollis Street, Emeryville, CA 94608. 510-547-4613. Subscriptions: 800-365-7773. $90/year (25 issues) sent 1st class; $34.95/year (25 issues) sent 3rd class.

Computer Gaming World   Best magazine for dedicated to fanatical computer game players. Published by Golden Empire Publications, Inc., 130 Chaparral Court, Suite 260, Anaheim Hills, CA 92808. Subscriptions: Computer Gaming World, P.O. Box 730, Yorba Linda, CA 92686-9963. 800-827-4450. $24/year (12 issues).

Computer Shopper   *Large format, very thick (800+ pages) magazine chock-full of product information. Great source of information on computer user groups and bulletin board systems (BBS)—each published alternate months. Most complete resource for by-mail shopping: hardware, software, supplies, and everything else you need. Check prices here before you go to computer stores. Published by Coastal Associates Publishing L.P., One Park Avenue, New York, NY 10016. Subscriptions: Computer Shopper, P.O. Box 51020, Boulder, CO 80321-1020. 800-274-6384. $29.97/year (12 issues)—blow-in card says $19.97.*

MicroTimes   Large-format magazine for somewhat experienced users. Available free at many computer stores in California. San Francisco Bay Area edition contains advertisements for local stores. Ask about it at your local computer stores or magazine stores. Good source of information on regional computer user groups and bulletin board systems (BBS). Published by BAM Publications, Inc., 3470 Buskirk Avenue, Pleasant Hill, CA 94523. Main office: 510-934-3700. Los Angeles: 213-467-7878. San Jose: 408-244-4400. Anaheim: 714-939-2809. Published every 2 weeks, 26 issues/year. Subscriptions: $29 for 13 issues sent 3rd class (allow 3-4 weeks delivery); $55 for 13 issues sent 1st class (allow 1-2 weeks delivery). Sample issue: $4.

One Thousand   Get this magazine if you have a Tandy 1000 series computer, if you use DeskMate on any PC, or if you are interested in learning how to use BASIC, the "people's programming language." Published by Symbiotics, Inc., P.O. Box 1688, Maryland Heights, MO 63043-0688. 314-521-9080. $24/year (12 issues).

PC Computing   General-purpose magazine, pitched at a more experienced audience than *PC Home Journal*. Regular departments called New!, Help, Consumer's Edge, and Prime Time. Prime Time includes Home Office, Games & Leisure, and Personal Finance. Our favorite general-purpose computer magazine for somewhat experienced users. Editorial office: 950 Tower Lane, Foster City, CA 94404. 415-578-7000. Subscriptions: PC/Computing, P.O. Box 58229, Boulder, CO 80322-8229. 800-365-2770. $29.97/year (12 issues)—blow-in card says $14.97.

PC Home Journal   *Recommended as the best general-purpose computer magazine for beginners. Published by Antic Publishing, 544 Second Street, San Francisco, CA 94107. PC Home Journal Subscriptions, P.O.Box 469, Mt. Morris, IL 61054. 815-734-6309 or 800-435-0715. Credit card subscriptions and sales: 800-234-7001. $14.95/year (12 issues).*

PC Sources   *Monthly with extensive product coverage and lots of advertisements. A good magazine for shoppers. Published by Coastal Associates Publishing, L. P., One Park Avenue, New York, NY 10016. Subscriptions: PC Sources, P.O. Box 53298, Boulder, CO 80322-3298. 800-827-2078. $16.97/year (12 issues)—blow-in card offer: $12.97.*

Shareware Magazine   *The number-one source for information about high-quality, low-cost shareware. Published six times/year by PC-SIG, 1030-D East Duane Avenue, Sunnyvale, CA 94086. PC-SIG membership costs $20/year and includes a 1-year subscription (6 issues) and other goodies. $39.95 membership includes magazine subscription, 5 shareware disks, and the* Encyclopedia of Shareware. *800-245-6717.*

Tightwad Computer Gazette   *For people who want to get the most while spending the least. For a free sample copy, send a self-addressed, stamped (29 cents) envelope to Tightwad Computer Gazette, P.O. Box 62, Graton, CA 95444.*

Books

Here is a listing of books that PC users will find helpful and informative.

Books for Older Versions of DOS

These books cover DOS Versions 2, 3, and 4. Be sure you get DOS books appropriate to the version of DOS on your computer.

Anis, Nick, and Craig Menefee. *PC User's Guide*. Superior beginner's to advanced intermediate book on installation and use of PCs. Excellent sections on selection and setup, with good overviews of available software. Published by Osborne/McGraw-Hill, 2600 Tenth Street, Berkeley, CA 94710. 800-227-0900. $29.95.

Bauer, Ron. *Easy DOS It!* Excellent introduction to DOS for users of PCs with floppy disks only (no hard disk). Published by Easy Way Press, Inc., P.O. Box 906, Rochester, MI 48308-0906. 313-651-9405. $6 plus $1.50 shipping/handling.

Jamsa, Kris. *Simply DOS*. Excellent beginner's book for users of PCs with hard disks (not appropriate for computer with floppy disks only—no hard disk). Published by Osborne/McGraw-Hill, 2600 Tenth Street, Berkeley CA 94710. 800-227-0900. $14.95.

A Book That Covers DOS 5.0

DOS 5.0 is the latest release of DOS for PCs.

Schildt, Herbert. *DOS 5 Made Easy*. Extensive tutorial on the latest version of DOS, DOS 5.0. Published by Osborne/McGraw-Hill, 2600 Tenth Street, Berkeley, CA 94710. 800-227-0900. $19.95.

GUI Books

These books will help you learn how to use DeskMate, GeoWorks, or Windows.

Byron, David and Herb Kraft. *Simply Windows*. Tells you how to get started using Microsoft's Windows GUI. Osborne/McGraw-Hill, 2600 Tenth Street, Berkeley, CA 94710. 800-227-0900. $14.95.

Nimersheim, Jack. *The First Book of GeoWorks Ensemble*. Published by SAMS/Macmillan Publishing Group, Front and Brown Streets, Riverside, NJ 08075. 800-257-5755.

Zamora, Ramon, and Bob Albrecht. *DeskMate 3 Made Easy*. Slow and easy task-oriented tutorial on Tandy's DeskMate. Published by Osborne/McGraw-Hill. Available from Play Together, Learn Together, P.O. Box 374, Coeur d'Alene, ID 83814. $19.95 plus $2 shipping and handling.

Books About Shareware

Shareware is a valuable resource for PC users. Here are a few books that deal with shareware.

Callahan, Mike, and Nick Anis. *Dr. File Finder's Guide to Shareware*. A book/disk package. The book is a tome, 1019 pages. Following page 1019 are dozens of pages of special offers. Open the back cover to find a disk containing some of Dr. File Finder's favorite shareware. Osborne/McGraw-Hill, 2600 Tenth Street, Berkeley, CA 94710. 800-227-0900. $39.95.

The PC-SIG Encyclopedia of Shareware. Descriptions of more than 1500 shareware disks. This is the authors' primary source of information about shareware. It is updated periodically as the shareware cornucopia expands. Published by PC-SIG, 1030-D East Duane Avenue, Sunnyvale, CA 94086. 800-245-6717. $19.95.

Zamora, Ramon, Frances Saito, and Bob Albrecht. *The Shareware Book*. Task-oriented tutorial book on the popular shareware applications: PC-Write (word processor), PC-File+ (database manager), and PC-Calc+ (spreadsheet). Published by Osborne/McGraw-Hill. Available from Play

Together, Learn Together, P.O. Box 374, Coeur d'Alene, ID 83814. $19.95 plus $2 shipping and handling.

PC Software
Companies

Here is a partial list of software development organizations and the names (in parentheses) of some of their programs. To help you gather information about PC software, write to these people and ask them to send you their catalogs and product information.

Adobe Systems, Inc., 1585 Charleston Road, Mountain View, CA 94039 (Adobe Illustrator, PhotoShop)

Aldus Corporation, 411 First Avenue South, Seattle, WA 98104 (Page-Maker)

Ashton-Tate Corporation, 20101 Hamilton Avenue, Torrance, CA 90502 (dBASE)

Autodesk, Inc., 2320 Marinship Way, Sausalito, CA 94965 (AutoCAD)

Borland International, 1700 Green Hills Road, Scotts Valley, CA 95066-0001 (Quattro Pro, Reflex)

Broderbund Software, Inc., 17 Paul Drive, San Rafael, CA 94903-2101 (Playroom, Where in the World Is Carmen Sandiego?)

Corel Systems, 1600 Carling Avenue, Ottawa, Ontario KIZ 8R7 (Corel Draw)

CrossTalk Communications, 1000 Holcomb Woods Parkway, Roswell, GA 30076-2575 (CrossTalk)

DataStorm Technologies, Inc., 1621 Towne Drive, Suite G, Columbia, MO 65202 (PROCOMM PLUS)

Generic Software, 11911 North Creek Parkway South, Bothell, WA 98011 (Generic CADD)

Hayes Microcomputer Products, Inc., 5923 Peach Tree Industrial Park Boulevard, Norcross, GA 30092 (SmartCom II)

Intuit, Inc., 540 University Avenue, Palo Alto, CA 94301 (Quicken)

Logitech, Inc., 6505 Kaiser Drive, Fremont, CA 94555 (Logitech Paint-show)

Lotus Development Corporation, 55 Cambridge Parkway, Cambridge, MA 01242 (Lotus 1-2-3, LotusWorks)

Micrografx, Inc., 1303 Arapaho, Richardson, TX 75081 (Micrografx Designer)

Microsoft Corporation, 16011 NE 36th Way, Redmond, WA 98073 (Excel, Microsoft Word, Microsoft Works, MS-DOS)

Sierra On-Line, Inc., Box 485, Coarsegold, CA 93614 (King's Quest Series)

Software Publishing Corporation, 1901 Landings Drive, Mountain View, CA 94039-7210 (PFS: First Choice, PFS: First Publisher, Professional Write)

Symantec Corporation, 10201 Torre Avenue, Cupertino, CA 95014 (Q&A)

Timeworks, Inc., 444 Lake Cook Road, Deerfield, IL 60015-4919 (Publish It!)

Ventura Software, Inc., 16160 Caputo Drive, Morgan Hill, CA 95037 (Ventura Publisher)

WordPerfect Corporation, 1555 North Technology Way, Orem, UT 84057 (WordPerfect)

WordStar International, 201 Alameda del Prado, Novato, CA 94949 (WordStar)

ZSoft Corporation, 450 Franklin Road, Suite 100, Marietta, GA 30067 (PC Paintbrush)

PC Hardware Vendors

This appendix contains a representative listing of companies that sell PC hardware systems. The listing is certainly not exhaustive. Look in your local telephone book (yellow pages) for additional vendors in your area.

National Computer Stores and Outlets

These national stores carry name-brand computers. These types of operations usually provide some form of full-service technical support and repairs.

CompuAdd, 12303 Technology Boulevard, Austin, TX 78727

ComputerLand Corporation, P.O. 9012, Pleasanton, CA 94566-9012

Sears, Sears Tower, Chicago, IL 60684

Tandy Corporation/Radio Shack, 1800 One Tandy Center, Fort Worth, TX 76102

Mail-order Operations

By-mail companies listed here provide (at least) 30-day money back, one-year warranty parts and labor, and toll-free telephone technical support. They usually have one or more pages of advertisements in magazines such as *Computer Shopper* and *PC Sources*. Put together the system you want and call for a price. If you don't have a particular system in mind, try the following minimum 386SX system:

386SX/16MHz (386SX CPU with a clock speed of 16 megahertz)

1MB (1 megabyte of memory)

1.44MB 3 1/2-inch FD (Floppy disk drive, stores 1.44 megabytes)

40MB (40 megabyte hard disk drive)

SVGA (Super VGA graphics card and monitor—800x600 or better)

Mouse or trackball

DOS 5.0

Or inquire about a minimum Windows system, like this one:

386SX/16MHz (386SX CPU with a clock speed of 16 megahertz)

2MB (2 megabytes of memory—also get prices for 4MB and 8MB)

1.44MB 3 1/2-inch FD (Floppy disk drive, stores 1.44 megabytes)

80MB (80 megabyte hard disk drive)

SVGA (Super VGA graphics card and monitor—800x600 or better)

Mouse or trackball

DOS 5.0 and Windows

Inquire about other goodies. Some companies throw in an integrated software package such as Microsoft Works or Lotus's LotusWorks.

Ares Microdevelopment, Inc., 24762 Crestview Court, Farmington Hills, MI 48018. 800-322-3200.

Dell Computer Corporation, 9505 Arboretum Boulevard, Austin, TX 78759-7299. 800-627-0440.

Gateway 2000, 610 Gateway Drive, N. Sioux City, SD 57049. 800-523-2000.

Leading Technology, Inc., 4685 South Ash Avenue, Suite H-5, Tempe, AZ 85282. 800-999-1973.

Northgate Computer Systems, Inc., 7075 Flying Cloud Drive, Eden Prairie, MN 55344. 800-828-6131.

Swan Technologies, 3075 Research Drive, State College, PA 16802. 800-468-9044.

Tri-Star Computer Corporation, 707 West Geneva, Tempe, AZ 85282. 800-678-2799.

USA Flex, 135 North Brandon Drive, Glen Ellyn, IL 60139. 800-872-3539.

ZEOS International, Ltd., 530 5th Avenue, N.W., St. Paul, MN 55112. 800-423-5891.

Remarketing Operations

Some companies specialize in the remarketing of used and discontinued PCs. Used equipment is often reconditioned and offered with a limited warranty. Discontinued equipment is purchased in bulk and resold at substantial discounts.

Tredex, 1875 Century Park East, Suite 2633, Los Angeles, CA 90067. 800-338-0939.

Boston Computer Exchange, Box 1177, Boston, MA 02103. 617-542-4414.

By-mail PC Peripherals and Supplies

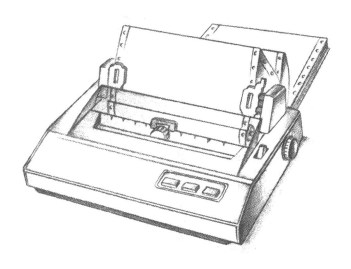

You can order PC peripherals and computer supplies through the mail. There are many reliable mail-order firms that specialize in providing fast service at minimum prices. Here are only a few of these types of businesses:

By-mail PC Peripherals

These three companies offer a good selection of PC peripherals. CAD and Graphics specializes in pointing devices, scanners, and high-resolution monitors.

CAD and Graphics, 1301 Evans Avenue, San Francisco, CA 94124. 800-288-1611.

Lyco, P.O. Box 5088, Jersey Shore, PA 17740. 800-233-8760.

Midwest Micro-Peripherals, 6910 U.S. Route 36 East, Fletcher, OH 45326. 800-423-8215.

By-mail PC Supplies

These three companies sell a variety of PC supplies. If you need disks in bulk or printer ribbons (Americal, MEI), disk storage units (Americal, National), or cables and surge protectors (National), these are the people to contact.

Americal Group, 12132 Sherman Way, North Hollywood, CA 91605. 800-288-8025.

MEI/Micro Center, 1100 Steelwood Road, Columbus, OH 43212. 800-634-3478.

National Computer Accessories, 769 North 16th Street, Suite 200, Sacramento, CA 95814-0527. 916-441-1568.

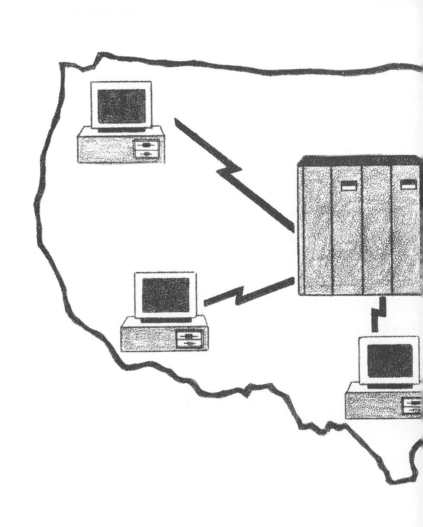

Information Services

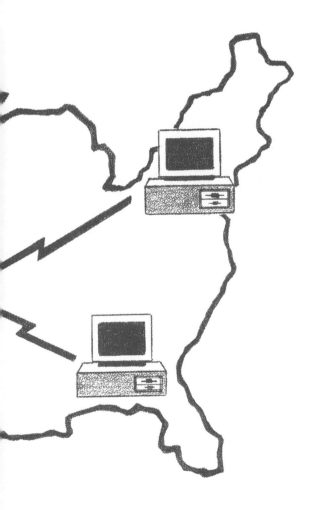

The following information services let you use your PC as an information-gathering system. From the comfort of your home or office, you can send electronic mail, chat electronically with people all around the world, enter into online discussion groups, play computer games, acquire software, make plane reservations, and look at stock quotations.

To perform these modern-day activities, you need a PC, a modem, a telephone, and a communications software program. The modem is a hardware device that helps your PC "talk," usually over telephone lines, to other PCs and computer systems. The communications program helps direct the sending and receiving of information that is passed through the modem.

CompuServe   5000 Arlington Centre Boulevard, Columbus, OH 43220. 800-848-8199. Startup: $39.95. Monthly minimum: $2.00. Price/hour: $12.50 prime time; $12.50 non-prime time. CompuServe is one of the biggest networks. It has the most users and a wide range of services. It also happens to be the most expensive. Before trying CompuServe, you may want to get some network experience on one of the less expensive systems, such as Prodigy or PC-Link.

Delphi   3 Blackstone Street, Cambridge, MA 02139. 800-544-4005. Startup: $49.95. Monthly minimum: $5.95 (Basic Plan); $20.00 (20/20 Advantage Plan). Price/hour, Basic Plan: $16.00 prime time; $6.00 non-prime time. Price/hour, 20/20 Advantage plan: $10.20 prime time; $1.20 non-prime time. Beginning information browsers may want to look at Prodigy and PC-Link before going online with Delphi.

GEnie   401 N. Washington Street, Rockville, MD 20850. 800-638-9636. Startup: free. Monthly minimum: $4.95. Some free services, including electronic mail (E-Mail), encyclopaedia, and some news and weather information. For additional services, price/hour: $18.00 prime time; $6.00 non-prime time.

PC-Link, Quantum Computer Services   8619 Westwood Center Drive, Vienna, VA 22182. 800-458-8532. Startup: free. Monthly minimum: $9.95 provides many basic services at no extra cost. System includes lots of shareware you can download to your computer. PC-Link Plus provides additional services, price/hour: $15.00 prime time; $6.00 non-prime time. For beginners, PC-Link provides a low-cost, easy-to-use introduction to an information service.

Prodigy   445 Hamilton Avenue, White Plains, NY 10601. 800-776-3449. Startup: $49.95. Monthly minimum: $12.95; Price/hour: free prime time; free non-prime time (exception: $.25 for each message after the first 30 messages in one month). Prodigy is the least expensive and easiest-to-use network. Recommended as the first network experience for neophytes.

Glossary of Terms

30386 monitor

disks

ot

clip art

3 1/2-inch Disk   A floppy disk. A circular piece of plastic material enclosed in a sturdy plastic case. Data is written onto and retrieved from the magnetic surface of the plastic disk.

5 1/4-inch Disk   A floppy disk. A circular piece of plastic material enclosed in a slightly flexible case.

9-pin Printer   A dot-matrix printer with a 9-pin printhead.

24-pin Printer   A dot-matrix printer with a 24-pin printhead.

286   Abbreviation for 80286 CPU.

386   Abbreviation for 80386 CPU.

386DX   Abbreviation for 80386DX CPU.

386SX   Abbreviation for 80386SX CPU.

486   Abbreviation for 80486 CPU.

8086   The code number for the Intel 8086 microprocessor. The first chip in the "86" series of CPUs.

8088   The code number for the Intel 8088 microprocessor. One of the oldest microprocessor chips.

80286   The code number for the Intel 80286 microprocessor. The second chip in the "86" series of CPUs.

80386   The code number for the Intel 80386 microprocessor. Sold in most of today's new PCs.

80386DX   An alternate designation for the 80386 CPU.

80386SX   A version of the 80386DX chip with fewer features.

80486   The code number for the Intel 80486 microprocessor. The latest in the series of "86" CPUs. The fastest and most powerful of today's microprocessors.

Algorithm   A set of steps or instructions designed to accomplish a task.

Alphanumeric Information   Information that contains both letters and numbers.

Application Software Programs   Programs designed to help PC users accomplish specific tasks such as word processing, creating graphics, and performing calculations.

Artificial Intelligence   A branch of computer science that deals with trying to simulate human thought processes with a computer. Abbreviated as AI.

AT Computer   An older PC that superseded the earlier XT models.

Auto-answer   A type of modem and software that automatically answers incoming calls.

Auto-dial   A type of modem and software that automatically dials telephone numbers.

Backward-compatible Program   A program that can use data files created by earlier versions of the same product.

Back Up   To make duplicate copies of programs or data files.

BASIC   A programming language. The letters in the name stand for Beginners All-purpose Symbolic Instruction Code.

BBS   Abbreviation for bulletin board system.

Binary Digit   Either a one (1) or a zero (0) as used in the binary number system. Also called a bit.

Bit   A binary digit.

Bit Rate   A measure of data transmission speed. Also stated in terms of bits per second (bps).

Board   A flat, stiff card on which electronic components are mounted.

Boot   To start up a PC system.

BPS   Bits per second. Shorthand notation for bit rate.

Bubble-jet Printer   A type of printer that prints on paper with ink particles that have been electrostatically charged.

Bug   An error that occurs in a software program. Ideally, good software programs are bug free.

Bulletin Board System   An electronic system composed of a computer, a modem, and software that lets users exchange information. Users access a BBS over telephone lines.

Bus Mouse   A type of mouse that connects to a board installed inside the PC.

Byte   One character of information (8 bits of data).

Cache Memory   PC memory that uses high-speed memory chips for the storage of frequently used data. Found in high performance PCs.

CAD Program   Computer-aided design software. Used by engineers and architects.

Card   A printed circuit board.

Cartridge Disk   A removable disk that stores large amounts of data.

CD Drive   A compact disc unit that uses either CD-ROMs or CD-I media.

CD-I   Compact Disc Interactive. A type of CD medium and player that lets the user interact with the stored information.

CD-ROM   Compact Disc Read-Only Memory. A type of CD medium and player that only lets a user read the stored information.

Central Processing Unit   The main integrated circuit in a PC. Performs the overall control of all the PC's functions and operations. Abbreviated as CPU.

CGA   Abbreviation for color graphics adapter.

Chassis   The housing, or case, of a PC.

Clip Art   Electronic art images that can be used instantly by anyone working with graphics software.

Cold Boot   The steps required to start up a PC, beginning with turning on the unit's power.

Color Graphics Adapter   A PC video mode that provides the lowest level of color graphics on a PC.

Compact Disc Drive A device that can play (read, write) compact discs (CD-I, CD-ROM).

Computer Program A set of instructions that tells the PC what to do.

Computer Programming Language Any language used by a programmer to create computer programs.

Copy-protected Software Software that has built-in protections against anyone making duplicates of the original disks.

CPS Abbreviation for characters per second. Normally applied to printer rates.

CPU Abbreviation for central processing unit.

Crash An unexpected, catastrophic failure of a software program or hardware device.

Cursor An indicator on the screen showing where the user's next action will take place.

Cursor Control Keys Sets of keys that control the movements of the cursor.

Cursor Control Keypad A cluster of cursor control keys on the keyboard.

Data A collection of characters or numbers.

Data File An organized set of data.

Database A collection of related data that has been organized for search and retrieval activities.

Database Management System   A software program designed to manage and manipulate a database of information. Abbreviated as DBMS.

DBMS   Abbreviation for database management system.

Debug   To test a computer program and eliminate bugs, or errors in the program.

Desktop Computer   A PC that sits on a desk or work table and is not easily portable. Contrasted with portable and laptop units.

Desktop Publishing   The process of using a PC to produce high-quality printed documents, including camera-ready materials. Enables you to merge and preview text and graphics on the PC screen before printing occurs.

Digital Electronic Circuitry   Electronic signals or data storage techniques that use only two information states, on and off. PCs rely heavily on digital electronic circuitry.

Digitizer   A scanner that converts images or text into digital information.

Directory   An index of files on a storage device.

Disk   The medium (floppy, hard, cartridge) or the hardware device that uses the medium.

Disk Cartridge   A removable disk that holds large amounts of information. Has the capacity advantages of a hard disk and the removable aspects of a floppy disk.

Disk Controller   A card or circuitry in the PC that controls the operations of the disk drives.

Disk Drive   A peripheral device that reads data from and writes data to disks.

Disk Operating System   The set of software programs that controls the basic operations of a PC. On the PC, there are two common operating systems, PC-DOS and MS-DOS. Abbreviated as DOS.

Diskette   A floppy disk. Often shortened to simply "disk."

Display Adapter   A board or circuitry in a PC that controls the type of display information on the monitor. The adapter converts the PC's digital signals into signals that can be understood by the monitor.

Documentation   The printed information that comes with a PC or software.

DOS   Abbreviation for disk operating system.

DOS Shell   A program that lets a user activate DOS commands from menus or lists.

Dot Pitch   A measure of how close together the color dots are on a monitor. Expressed in millimeters; the smaller the value, the better the resolution of the monitor.

Dot-matrix Printer   A printer with a printhead that has a matrix of small pins. It prints characters by selecting combinations of pins and striking the printhead against the paper.

Download   To move a file electronically from an external computer into a PC.

Draw Program   A type of graphics program that creates final images by overlaying combinations of objects (lines, curves, solids, shapes).

DTP   Abbreviation for desktop publishing.

Edit   To alter a document or image.

EGA   An enhanced graphics adapter.

Electronic Mail   Communications that are transmitted and received by using PCs and other computers.

Enhanced Graphics Adapter   A video standard introduced to provide greater resolution and more colors than earlier PC graphics modes such as CGA. Abbreviated as EGA.

Ergonomic Features   Design features that account for the way humans think, move, and are built to allow people to use software and equipment more efficiently and with greater comfort.

Expansion Board   A circuit board that expands the capabilities of a PC.

Expansion Slot   A slot in the PC chassis to house an expansion board.

External Storage Devices   Any data storage device that sits outside the PC chassis.

Fatal Error   A catastrophic error that happens while you are running a software program. Also called a crash of the system.

Fax   Abbreviation for facsimile; the electronic transmission of documents.

File   A collection of data on a disk or other medium. Each file is identified by a filename.

Filename   The name of a file on a disk or other medium.

Firmware   Software that has been converted into circuitry on a chip.

Fixed Disk   Another name for a hard disk.

Flat-bed Scanner   A type of scanner that lets you scan entire pages of information in one pass.

Floppy Disk   Any of the various types of smaller, removable disks used on a PC.

Font   A collection of characters that appears on the screen or page in one typeface.

Form Letters   Documents in which selected parts are changed by the software as the letter is printed.

Footprint   The amount of space taken up by a PC as it sits on a flat surface.

Fractal   A mathematical object that can be used to create interesting graphics images.

Freeware   A type of user-supported software. "Freeware" is a copyrighted term owned by Headlands Press.

Friction Feed   On printers, the method of paper movement that relies on the pressure of a roller against the paper.

Function Keys   A set of keys on the keyboard that change function based on the software being used.

Gigabyte   Approximately one billion bytes or a thousand megabytes.

Graphical User Interface   A style of software interface that lets users interact with programs visually. Referred to as a GUI (pronounced "gooey"), this type of interface relies on icons and images rather than on command-type interactions.

Graphics   Images, as opposed to text and numbers.

Graphics Board   A circuit board that controls a PC's graphics capabilities.

Graphics Printer   Any printer that supports graphical output.

Graphics Tablet   A sensitized tablet that a user can draw on to create images on the PC's screen.

GUI   Abbreviation for graphical user interface.

Hand-held Scanner   A scanning unit that fits in, and is controlled by, the hand.

Hard Copy   The printed output from a computer.

Hardcard   A hard disk that is mounted on a circuit board and fits into an expansion slot within the PC chassis.

Hard Disk   An auxiliary storage device with a fixed, and usually non-removable magnetic disk component.

Hardware   The collection of electronic devices that make up a PC. Hardware includes chips, keyboards, disk drives, the chassis, the monitor, printers, scanners, and pointing devices.

Hertz   A measure of cycles per second. One hertz equals 1 cycle per second (cps).

High Resolution A measure of sharpness and clarity of images on a monitor, as contrasted with low or medium resolution units.

Hz Abbreviation for hertz.

IBM-compatible Any PC that matches the features and capabilities of a standard IBM PC.

Icon A graphics image that represents an object, program, or feature.

Impact Printer Any printer in which the printhead strikes the paper.

Ink-jet Printer A printer that directs tiny, electrostatically-charged ink particles onto the paper. Also see Bubble-jet printer.

Integrated Circuit A collection of interconnected electronic components, mounted on a single chip, designed to perform a set of specified functions.

Integrated Software Package Any software package that combines one or more programs into a single system in which data files can easily be exchanged between program units.

Interface The communication boundary between two dissimilar processes; for example, the interface created by a programmer between the program and the user who plans to use the package.

I/O Abbreviation for Input/Output.

Joystick A pointing device used primarily with entertainment packages.

KB Abbreviation for kilobyte.

Key   Any of the buttons on the surface of a keyboard.

Keyboard   A collection of keys mounted into a single unit. The PC keyboard is the primary input device to a PC program.

Kilobyte   Approximately 1000 bytes or characters of data. Abbreviated as KB.

Laptop Computer   A smaller, lighter-weight version of the desktop computer, which can be carried to different locations.

Laser Printer   A high-quality printing device that can produce camera-ready documents.

Letter-quality   Describes a printer that produces output that looks as good as or better than a typewritten document. Abbreviated as LQ.

Light Pen   A pointing device that users can touch to the monitor's screen to make selections.

Load   To bring information into the PC's memory.

LQ   Abbreviation for letter-quality.

MB   Abbreviation for megabyte.

MDA   Abbreviation for monochrome display adapter.

Megabyte   Approximately 1 million bytes of data. Abbreviated as MB.

Megahertz   One million hertz or one million cps. Abbreviated as MHz.

Memory   That part of the PC in which information is temporarily stored until it is needed by the computer's CPU.

Menu   A set of options arranged in a list.

MHz   Abbreviation for megahertz.

Microcomputer   Another name for a PC.

Microprocessor   The type of chip found inside the PC; the CPU.

Microsecond   One millionth of a second.

Millisecond   One thousandth of a second.

Modem   A device that translates digital signals from the PC into signals that can be transmitted over telephone lines. This unit also decodes incoming signals back into data that can be handled by a PC.

Monitor   The display screen of a PC.

Mono   Abbreviation for monochrome.

Mono/VGA   Shorthand notation for a display adapter that handles only monochrome images but at VGA resolutions.

Monochrome Display Adapter   The form of PC video display that uses only two colors (white on black, white on green, and so on). Often abbreviated as MDA.

Monochrome Monitor   A monitor that displays in only two colors (white on black, white on green, etc.)

Motherboard   The main circuit board in a PC, to which other components are attached.

Mouse   A pointing device that rolls around on a flat surface. The movement of the mouse is translated on the screen into movements of the cursor.

Mouse Pad   A textured, rectangular pad on which you can roll a mouse.

MS-DOS   The Microsoft disk operating system.

Multiscanning Monitor   A monitor that looks at incoming video signals and adjusts the display to accommodate the signals being received.

Multitasking   The ability to operate more than one program at the same time.

Near-letter-quality   Describes a printer that produces output of lesser quality than a typewritten document. Abbreviated as NLQ.

NLQ   Abbreviation for near-letter-quality.

Non-impact Printer   A printer that does not print by having a printhead strike the paper. Examples are bubble-jet and laser printers.

Notebook Computer   A lightweight (4 to 7 pounds) PC about the size of a notebook or binder.

Numeric Keypad   The cluster of keyboard keys that simulates the ten-key pad on a calculator.

OCR   Abbreviation for optical character recognition.

Operating Environment   The software environment within which software programs operate. Can also refer to a DOS shell or to a GUI.

Operating System   Usually, the disk operating system (DOS). The two most common operating systems are PC-DOS and MS-DOS. Abbreviated as OS.

Optical Character Recognition   The ability of software and hardware to scan text and convert the images into characters that can be used by a word processing program. Abbreviated as OCR.

OS   Abbreviation for operating system.

Paint Program   A software package that lets a user paint images on the screen with a set of paint tools (brushes, spray cans, shape-makers, and textures). Paint programs let users control each pixel (dot) on the screen.

Parallel Port   A port on a PC that transmits several bits of information simultaneously.

PC   Abbreviation for personal computer. Refers to both IBM PCs and IBM-compatibles.

PC-compatible   Another term for IBM-compatible; PCs that provide the features and functionality of the standard IBM PCs.

PC-DOS   The disk operating system provided by IBM.

PCL   The printer control language found on Hewlett-Packard laser printers.

Pen and Tablet   A pointing device system that lets users draw with a pen on the surface of a sensitized tablet.

Peripherals   Any of the devices that attach to a PC (printers, keyboards, monitors, pointing devices, and external storage units).

Peripheral Devices   Same as peripherals.

Personal Computer   The small, powerful microcomputers also referred to as PCs.

Pin-feed Printer   A printer that uses a tractor with a set of pins to move paper through the unit.

Pixel   The smallest dot on the screen of a PC.

Point Size   The size of a character.

Pointing Device   Any device (mouse, trackball, joystick, pen and tablet) that attaches to a PC and is used to control actions on the screen.

PostScript   The laser printer control language developed by Adobe Systems.

Port   An outlet on a PC where a peripheral device cable can be attached.

Portable Computer   Any PC that can be carried easily from place to place.

Printer   A PC peripheral that creates printed documents from the information being processed by the computer.

Printer Control Language   A specialized language that controls the operations of the more sophisticated laser printers.

Printhead   On impact printers, the part of the mechanism that strikes the paper to produce characters and images.

Program   A set of instructions that tells the PC what to do; also, the act of creating a program.

Programmer   A person who writes or creates programs.

Public Domain Software   Software that has been created and made available, at no charge, to the general public.

RAM   Random-access memory. That part of the PC's memory in which information is stored temporarily when the PC is turned on. When the PC is turned off, data stored in RAM disappears.

Resolution   The sharpness and clarity of images on a PC monitor; also, the number of dots per inch of images on a screen or on the printed page.

ROM   Read-only memory. That part of a PC's memory that permanently contains program instructions and data. The contents of ROM do not disappear when the PC is turned off.

Scanner   A device that converts text and graphics on paper into files that can be used by a computer.

Serial Mouse   A mouse that connects to one of the serial ports on the PC.

Serial Port   A port of the PC that transmits information one bit at a time.

Shareware   A type of user-supported software that users get to "try before they buy." Shareware authors are supported by voluntary user registration fees paid directly to the programs' creators.

Sharpness   On monitors, the aspect that relates to how fuzzy or clear an image appears.

Sheet Feeder   A tray or other device that feeds paper one sheet at a time into a printer.

Shell   A program that lets users interact with a PC by using a set of lists, or menus, instead of having to type commands from the keyboard.

Slot   A place to put a circuit board inside the PC chassis.

Software   A collection of programs that has been designed to make a PC perform tasks.

Software License Agreement   The agreement that comes with a software package. The agreement spells out your rights and the distributor's limits of liability.

Sound Board   A circuit board that adds sound and music features to the PC.

Sound Baffle   An enclosure to minimize the noise of impact printers.

Sound Synthesizer   The circuits and software that generate electronic sounds and music.

Spreadsheet   An application program that assists users with calculations.

Store   To save data onto a disk or other medium or in the PC's memory.

Stylus   A pencil-like device used with tablet systems for drawing images.

Surge Suppressor   An electrical connector that can minimize minor power fluctuations into a PC and disconnect the PC or PC peripherals completely if a large power surge occurs.

Super VGA   A video mode that provides extra high-resolution images. Abbreviated as SVGA.

System Utilities Programs that come with the operating system that help users manage and maintain their PCs.

Tablet A sensitized device that users draw on when creating images on the screen.

Tape Backup System A data storage device used to back up hard disks onto high-capacity tape cassettes.

Telecommunications Program A program that lets users communicate with each other through their PCs by using modems and telephone lines.

Trackball A stationary pointing device operated with the fingers or thumb.

Tractor Feed On printers, a mechanism that uses pins to move paper though the device.

Typeface The name of a particular font, usually designated by the person who creates the typeface.

Upgrade To exchange an older version of a product for a newer version.

Upload To send information electronically from your PC to another PC or computer.

Video Graphics Adapter A moderately high-resolution video system for displaying PC images.

VGA Abbreviation for video graphics adapter.

Voice Recognition Device   Software and hardware that can identify components of a user's spoken utterances.

Voice Synthesizer   Software and hardware that can mimic or reproduce the human voice.

Warm Boot   The steps involved in restarting a PC without having to turn off its power.

Window   A section of a display that encloses a particular set of information.

Word Processor   A program that lets users create, edit, format, and print documents that contain both text and graphics.

Word Wrap   In a word processor, the feature that automatically moves words to the next line so that the text fits on the screen.

WYSIWYG   Acronym for "What You See Is What You Get." A concept that emerged with the development of sophisticated desktop publishing programs that allows users to preview on the screen what the program will print on the printer.

XT Computer   An early form of PC that is now considered "dinosaur" technology.

Index

K

L

M

Q